THE GOLDEN AGE OF COOKERY

THE GOLDEN AGE
OF COOKERY

by

TOM BRIDGE

Ross Anderson Publications

Published in 1983 by
Ross Anderson Publications
22 Higher Dunscar
Egerton
Bolton
BL7 9TE

© Tom Bridge 1983

British Library Cataloguing in Publication Data
 Bridge, Tom
  The Golden age of Cookery
  1. Cookery – History
  I. Title
  641.5'09   TX651

ISBN 0-86360-008-5

Photoset in Times by
Action Typesetting, Gloucester
and printed in Great Britain by
Billings of Worcester

By the same author
THE PEOPLE OF BOLTON ON COOKERY

ACKNOWLEDGMENTS

I would like to thank historian and author Mr Derek Billington for his help and encouragement; Mr Joe Hyam and all the staff of *The Caterer & Hotelkeeper* for the use of extracts from *Caterer & Hotelkeeper* 1878; Mr Thorn and Mr A. G. Costa, Chairman, both of Keddie Ltd for the use of the Geo. Watkins labels; Mr Norman Slark for the loan of material in the book; Mr Chris Driver and The Bolton Museum for the loan of their books; *The Bolton Evening News* and *Bolton Chronicle* for their invaluable help in getting some of the old recipes; my good friend Martin Scott for letting me get on with the book, while other business prevailed; Mr Michael Malone without whose help and hard work this book would not have been possible; Sonia Cohen, Carnes Hotel & Catering Agency, 26 Brown Street, Manchester; Donald Tonge for his advice and help on photographs and prints; Bill Broadbent, Custodian of Hall-ith-Wood Museum, Bolton for all his help.

Contents

LIST OF ILLUSTRATIONS

LIST OF CARTOONS

All the above cartoons drawn by Hannah Firmin.

Introduction

Think how many great chefs came to this country in the nineteenth century, such as Escoffier, Careme, Soyer and Brillat-Savarin, who wrote their influence into the cookery books of today. They came here because English food and traditional recipes are worth writing down.

I have compiled for you some of the great recipes of that golden era when food was not frozen, pre-packed or convenience food. The range is from simple to grand, with a few modern recipes that are sensible and delicious.

The British have a great love of food, with a home-bred tradition that the Europeans are now following. It is Rosa Lewis who inspired the TV series, *The Duchess of Duke Street,* and Mrs Beeton still has the biggest following throughout the world with all housewives.

I have added tributes in this book to all the above people and more, because I too enjoy food and I want to share this little piece of history with you.

Brillat-Savarin declared that "The discovery of a new dish does more for the happiness of the human race than the discovery of a new star," and if *The Golden Age of Cookery* should encourage the cooks, chefs, housewives and students to build on standard recipes and invent better dishes, it has been well worth the two years spent writing it.

Tom Bridge.

William Kitchener *(National Portrait Gallery)*

Chapter 1
Cookery Books

There was writing on cookery before the nineteenth century. The earliest English cookery book seems to be one which was written by chief master cooks of Richard II in the late fourteenth century, *The Forme of Cury*. Compare one of the recipes in that book with some of the nineteenth century recipes which we shall be looking at later.

Cok A Grees
Take and make the self fars; but do thereto pyn and sug. Take an hole raosted cok, pulle hy and hylde him al togg'd, saue the legg. Take a pigg and hilde hy fro the mydd' donward, fylle hi ful of the fars and sowe hy fast toged. Do hy in a panne and seethe hy wel, and when thei bene isode, do he on a spyt and rost it wele. Colo it wi zolkes of ayren and safron. Lay theron foyles of gold and of silu, sue hit forth.

I would translate this recipe as follows:—

Cock and Wild Pig
Make some stuffing and put to one side.
Take a whole roast cock and pull it to pieces.
Put it together with the stuffing, but save the leg.
Take a pig and cut him down the stomach.
Fill it with the stuffing, and sew it up.
Put it in a pan and seal it, then when it is sealed
Put it on a spit and roast it well.
Colour it with the yolks of egg and saffron.
Lay it on a bed of leaves of silver and gold and serve.

It is interesting also to note the prices regulated by law in 1315:—

Edwarde by the grace of God Kynge of England &c. To Shiriffes, Majors, Bailiffes of Fraunchises Greeting: For as much as we have heard and understanded the greevous complayntes of Archbishops, Bishops, Prelates and Barons, touching great dearth of victuals in our Realme: We ordeyne from henceforth that no Oxe stalled or corne fedde be sold for more than xxixs. No other grass fed Oxe for more than xvis.; a fat stalled Cowe at xiis.; another Cowe lesse worth at xs.; a fat mutton corne fedde or whose wool is well growen at xxd.; another fat Mutton shorne at xiiiid.; a fat Hogge of two yeres olde at iiis. iiiid.; a fat Goose at iid.; ob.; in the Citie at iiid.; a fat Capon at iid.; in the Citie iid.; ob.; a fat Hen at id.; in the Citie at id.; two Chickens id.; in the Citie at id. ob.; foure Pigions id.; in the Citie three Pigions id. ob.; Item xxiiii Egges a peny, in the Citie xx Egges a peny. We ordeyne to all our Shiriffes.

I would presume *ob* means obligatory (imposing an obligation/binding).

3

Until the nineteenth century most books were written by cooks or housewives, who, skilled only in their own art, lacked the power of language to convey their knowledge clearly to others. Their books, ill spelt and ill expressed, were of no great use to the reader. But by and by a better style of cookery book appeared. Mrs Glasses bade us "first catch our hare" but nevertheless gave intelligible instructions as to what to do with it when caught. Dr Kitchener's excellent cookery book followed. Mrs Rundle became the guide of inexperienced housekeepers; William Street's *The Frugal Housewife*, printed by Russell & Allen of Manchester in 1811, is a beautiful cookery book which outlined everything the housewife should know about that period. Then there are all the classics such as Frederick Warne's *Model Cookery & Housekeeping Book* 1868, which I have a first edition of myself, Mrs Beeton's, Escoffier, down to our present day, Hering's Dictionary, Delia Smith, Katie Stewart, Robert Carrier and Michael Smith.

And as the art improves, books on the subject grow with it, nor need we wonder at the interest which these works possess for the public, when we consider the importance of gastronomy. Digestion, potent in its effects on the mind as well as on the body, depends greatly on the cooking of our food; and whoever can give a hint by which our viands may be rendered more palatable and nourishing, should be considered as a benefactor to his fellow-humans. Who shall say, how much of the gloom — spleen old writers called it — of our Anglo-Saxon character may have arisen from the heavy, strangely compounded, ill dressed food of our ancestors?

Mrs Isabella Beeton

Isabella was born Isabella Mayson on 14th March 1836, fifteen months before Victoria was Queen. Some twenty six years later she published with the help of her husband Samuel Beeton *The Book of Household Management,* 1861.

What an impression she made on the housewives and cooks of the Victorian era. She told her readers the duties of the Housekeeper, Kitchen maid, Cook, Footman, Butler, Valet, Coachman, Upper and Under Housemaids, Lady's Maid, Maid of all Work, Nurse and Nurse Maid, Monthly, Wet and Sick Nurses, Laundry Maid, and gave helpful information on all domestic problems, comfort and home life in general. Yet she probably never even boiled an egg herself. Sadly she died at the tender age of 28 a week after giving birth to a son on February 6th 1865.

Mrs Beeton *(National Potrait Gallery)*

The death of Isabella was a stunning blow to Samuel Beeton. Within months he was facing failure and bankruptcy was just around the corner. He was forced to dispose of his copyrights to a rival firm Ward, Lock and Tyler, of Paternoster Row. His most valuable asset *The Book of Household Management* went with everything else. Only his two sons brought him comfort but that was not to be for long. He died June 6th 1877 and was buried with the woman he loved so much, Isabella.

Ward and Lock soon recognised the value of the book. By 1890 it had sold over half a million copies. Mrs Beeton's today is still a top selling book.

From Mrs. Beeton's *Everyday Cookery* 1876
> Her Hand has lost its cunning — the firm, true hand that wrote these formulae, and penned the information contained in this little book.
>
> Cold in the silent tomb lie the once nimble, useful fingers, now nerveless, unable for anything, and ne'er to do work more in this world!
>
> Exquisite palate, unerring judgment, sound commonsense, refined tastes, — all these had the dear Lady who has gone ere her youth had scarcely come.
>
> But four times seven years were all she passed in this world; and since the day she became wedded wife — now nearly nine years past — her greatest, chiefest aims were to provide for the comfort and pleasure of those she loved and had around her, and to employ her best faculties for the use of her sisters, Englishwomen generally.
>
> Her surpassing affection and devotion led her to find her happiness in aiding, with all her heart and soul, the husband whom she richly blessed and honoured with her abounding love.
>
> Her works speak for themselves; and although taken from this world in the very height of health and strength, and in the early days of womanhood, she felt that satisfaction — so great to all who strive with good intent and warm will — of knowing herself regarded with respect and gratitude.

Jean Anthelme Brillat-Savarin (1755-1826)
Brillat-Savarin was born at Belley, France in 1755. He started his career as a lawyer and became Mayor of his town and commander of the National Guard in 1793. During the Reign of Terror he was banished and fled to Switzerland. He then spent nearly three years in America as a refugee before returning to France in 1797.

For nearly 25 years he worked on his *Physiologie du Gout, ou meditations de gastronomie transcendante,* which he wrote in two volumes, and this was published shortly before his death in Paris in 1826. The great chefs of Europe still quote him to this day.

Dr William Kitchener (1775-1827)
Dr William Kitchener was a great warm-hearted and amusing man,

Brillat-Savarin *(B.B.C. Hulton Picture Library)*

which can be seen in his *Apicius Redivivus,* or *The Cook's Oracle* which was one of the more eccentric of the cookery books of the early 19th century (1817). He was the life and soul of all his own parties at Fitzroy Square & Bloomsbury where he entertained weekly to his select circle of friends. If any of his guests were more than one minute late for dinner, they would be refused entry to the house. He was a great lover of food and a man whom I would have enjoyed dining with because of his eccentric moods and humour.

Here are Dr Kitchener's Rules for Marketing (1817):—

> The best rule for marketing is to pay ready money for everything, and to deal with the most respectable tradesmen in your neighbourhood. If you leave it to their integrity to supply you with a good article at the fair market price, you will be supplied with better provisions, and at as reasonable a rate as those bargain-hunters who trot "around, around, around about" a market till they are trapped to buy some unchewable old poultry, tough tup-mutton, stringy cow-beef, or stale fish, at a very little less than the price of prime and proper food.
>
> With savings like these they toddle home in triumph, cackling all the way, like a goose that has got ankle-deep into good luck. When you order meat, poultry, or fish, tell the tradesman when you intend to dress it: he will then have it in his power to serve you with provision that will do him credit, which the finest meat, &c., in the world will never do, unless it has been kept a proper time to be ripe and tender.

Eliza Acton (1799-1859)

Eliza Acton was a woman who knew about writing, whether it be poetry or the culinary arts. What she wrote was gospel to the housewife of the mid-nineteenth century. Born in Battle, Sussex, she was the daughter of John Acton, a local brewer who had a business in the scenic town of Hastings. Later the Acton family moved to Ipswich. From there she was sent to the South of France at the age of 25 as her health was not good (consumption of the lungs). After a fleeting romance with an Officer of the French Army she returned to England to live with her sister Sarah. She began to write poetry, not being very succesful in this field. She moved to Tonbridge, Kent in 1837 where she swotted away at the art of cookery until 1845, when her now famous book the *Modern Cookery in all Branches* was published. She was a woman who loved puddings, pastry and pancakes. Everything she did was accurate and precise to every detail.

Eliza's work was now getting the praise she deserved. She wrote *The English Bread Book,* which again was devoted to the housewife and showed how to make homemade dishes such as Sally Lunns, Oatmeal Bannocks and other bread dishes of that period. At the age of 58 she became very ill and in March 1859 died of cancer.

Here are Eliza Acton's Observations on omelettes, pancakes and fritters, taken from *The English Bread Book:*—

There is no difficulty in making good omelettes, pancakes, or fritters; and, as they may be expeditiously prepared and served, they are often a very convenient resource when, on short notice, an addition is required to a dinner.

The eggs for all of them should be well and lightly whisked; the lard for frying batter should be extremely pure in flavour, and quite hot when fritters are dropped in; the batter itself should be smooth as cream, and it should be briskly beaten the instant before it is used. All fried pastes should be perfectly drained from the fat before they are served, and sent to the table promptly when they are ready. Eggs may be dressed in a multiplicity of ways, but are seldom more relished in any form than in a well-made and expeditiously served omelette. This may be plain, or seasoned with minced herbs and a very little shallot, when the last is liked, and is then called Omelettes aux fines herbes; or it may be mixed with minced ham or grated cheese: in any case it should be thick, full-tasted, and fried only on one side; if turned in the pan, as it frequently is in England, it will at once be flattened and rendered tough. Should the slight rawness, which is sometimes found in the middle of the inside when the omelette is made in the French way, be objected to, a heated shovel, or a salamander (grill), may he held over it for an instant, before it is folded on the dish. The pan for frying it should be quite small; for if it be composed of four or five eggs only, and then put into a large one, it will necessarily spread over it and be thin, which would render it more like a pancake than an omelette; the only partial remedy for this, when a pan of proper size cannot be had, is to raise the handle of it high, and keep the opposite side to the fire, which will confine the eggs into smaller space.

Did you notice how much detail Eliza goes into to make sure everything is right?

Chapter 2
Eggs and Omelettes

The eggs of reptiles, fish and birds can all be used as food. Hens' eggs are the most used of all eggs. There are twelve basic methods.

1. Omelette, which I shall show you basic recipes for in this Chapter (7 and 8).
2. Scrambled eggs; first melt the butter in a shallow pan, add well beaten eggs, seasoned mixed with ¾ cup of milk to every 3 eggs, cook slowly whisking until they are congealed, keeping the eggs soft.
3. Soft boiled eggs, cook in boiling water for 3 minutes.
4. Medium boiled eggs, cook in boiling water for 5 minutes.
5. Hard boiled eggs, cook in boiling water for 10 minutes, hold under cold water for 3 minutes.
6. Eggs en cocotte, grease small to medium fire-proof china pot (cocotte) with butter, break an egg into it, salt and pepper the egg whites and cook in the oven.
7. Poached eggs, half fill a shallow pan with water and a little vinegar, bring the water to boil and slide the eggs into the water and poach for 4 minutes.
8. Moulded eggs, grease a mould with butter, break into the mould and poach in a tray of hot water, the same way as eggs en cocotte. Serve on a pastry tray.
9. Stuffed eggs, boil the eggs for 10 minutes (boiled eggs hard) cut the eggs crosswise, remove the yolk, mash and mix with mayonnaise or any other stuffing.
10. Fried eggs, grease a pan and fry the egg avoiding spoiling the yolk.
11. Baked eggs, heat the oil in a frying pan, drop the egg into the centre and shape with a spoon, the centre should remain soft, serve with a sauce.
12. Cold eggs, hard boiled coated with mayonnaise, glazed in aspic, en croutons or chaudfroid and garnished as desired.

If I wrote a book on eggs it would consist of 1,600 recipes which would be the extended versions of the above basic recipes. Here are a few from the 19th century.

1. Eggs en Cocotte with Tarragon

Cook the eggs as described above under Eggs en cocotte. When the eggs are cooked, pour a ring of concentrated veal gravy flavoured with tarragon round the yolks. Garnish with blanched tarragon leaves, arranged in a rose shape.

2. Delmonica Eggs (poached)

Coat the eggs with cheese sauce, mixed with chopped truffles, put them on a bed of noodles filled with lambs' sweetbreads and mushrooms, blended with Madeira sauce.

3. Mornay Eggs (soft boiled)

Arrange the cooked eggs in a fireproof dish on a layer of mornay sauce. Cover with mornay sauce. Sprinkle with grated cheese and melted butter. Brown in the top of the oven.

4. Prince of Wales (cold eggs)

2 large tomatoes cut in half and hollowed out, marinated in vinegar and olive oil, stuffed with salad of diced stalk celery, half a hard-boiled cold egg placed on each tomato, coated with mayonnaise.

5. Amulet of Asparagus (1806)

Beat up six eggs with cream, boil some of the large and finest asparagus.

When boiled, cut off all the green in small pieces. Mix them with the eggs and put in some pepper and salt. Make a slice of butter hot in the pan, put them in, and serve them on buttered toast.

6. Plovers' Eggs

Plovers' eggs must be boiled hard and served either hot or cold. For breakfast, line a little basket with moss and lay them in it after bringing to the boil for three minutes. If you have no basket, serve them on a folded table napkin, or shell them and pour béchamel sauce over them.

You may manufacture a satisfactory basket for plovers' eggs, by lining one of the round baskets in which strawberries are sold with moss, both outside and inside, and bending a twig over it for a handle.

7. Ham or Tongue Omelette or Amulet (1811)

Five ounces of butter, six eggs, a little pepper and salt, three dessertspoonfuls of grated ham or tongue.

Grate a little dressed ham or tongue very fine, fry it for two or three minutes in a piece of butter, put yolks of egg (six) and the whites of three eggs into a plate, season with a little salt and pepper, and beat it well until very light and smooth; stir in the grated ham or tongue. Put some butter into an omelette-pan, and when it begins to bubble, whirl up the mixture, and pour into the pan, stir it with a spoon one way until it thickens and becomes warm, and then fold the edges of the omelette over in an oval form. Brown it nicely, and serve as quickly as possible as the lightness of an omelette is spoilt unless it is served immediately.

8. Ham Amulet (1811)

3 large fresh eggs, (separated), ¼ lb very finely chopped York ham, ½ cup of fresh cream, 3 tablespoons of butter, salt and ground black pepper to taste.

Separate the eggs, and beat the yolks well, add salt and freshly ground black pepper, beat in the cream. Then beat in the egg whites till they are stiff but soft. Fold the whites into the yolks very very lightly. Heat an omelette pan 7 to 8 inches in diameter until hot, then add the butter, let it melt quickly but not brown, add the omelette mixture until half cooked then add the ham, place under a hot grill until it rises then serve with sprinkled parsley.

Eggs as a main course, except at the breakfast table, have never become established in England as they have in France or the States, that was until the omelette. The French had the flat omelette whilst the good old British fluffy omelette or souffle omelette started on the top of the stove and finished under the grill.

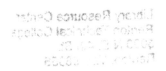

Chapter 3
The Gentleman's Breakfast and its Cost

Game was seen regularly on the nineteenth century Englishman's table for breakfast. Our breakfast in contrast is orange juice or cereal and boiled egg or egg and bacon with coffee or tea.

Breakfast in a gentleman's home in 1810
The table would have a snowy white linen tablecloth. Fresh flowers and fruit would adorn the table. The silver would be gleaming, tea, coffee and cocoa would be freshly made and very hot. At the head of the table breakfast cups and saucers — coffee cups to the right and tea cups to the left. The coffee pot and tea pot would stand in front of the urn, a slop-basin and milk jug, cream and hot milk all neatly together. Hot rolls in napkins, hot toast, bread on a wooden platter. On the sideboard would be large joints of cold ham, beef, pheasant, game pie, plovers eggs, hot plates of bacon chops and kidneys, with kippers. Eggs poached, scrambled or fried all done to order. The bread would have been baked fresh in a brick oven.

A breakfast for 14 people would have cost a little over a pound including the cook's wages, but a £1 a day every day was still a great deal of money. A poor family could live off that £1 for at least a month. Here are four samples of breakfast menus from Mrs Beeton's *Household Management*.

Breakfast for Twelve persons — Summer

1.	Menu	Average Cost s.d.	2.	Menu	Average Cost s.d.
	Fried Soles	3. 6.		Turbot a la Creme	2. 6.
	Ragout of Duck	3. 0.		Lamb Cutlets &	
				Mashed Potatoes	2. 9.
	Veal Pie	4. 0.		Croquettes of Beef	2. 0.
	Cold Chicken	3. 6.		Chaudfroid of	
				Chicken	4. 0.
	Tongue	2. 0.		Eggs	1. 3.
	Poached and Boiled			Ham	2. 0.
	Eggs	1. 3.		Cherries &	
	Strawberries	2. 0.		Raspberries	2. 0.
	Tea, Coffee, Hot			Tea, Coffee, Hot	
	& Cold Milk	1. 6.		& Cold Milk	1. 6.
	Bread Rolls, Toast			Bread & Butter	2. 6.
	& Butter	2. 6.			
	Total	**£1.3.3d**		**Total**	**£1. 0. 6d**

Breakfast for Twelve Persons — Winter

3.	Menu	Average Cost s. d.	4.	Menu	Average Cost s. d.
	Angels on Horseback	3. 9.		Rissoles of Fish	2. 0.
	Broiled Soles	3.6.		Broiled Kidneys	2. 6.
	Devilled Turkey	1. 6.		Salmi of Game	2. 0.
	Grilled Steak	2. 6.		Cold Grouse	4. 0.
	Game Pie	5. 0.		Cold Beef and Ham	3. 0.
	Cold Ham	2. 0.		Savoury Omelette	1. 9.
	Eggs	1. 3.		Tea, Coffee & Milk	1. 6.
	Tea, Coffee, Hot			Bread & Butter	2. 6.
	& Cold Milk	1. 6.			
	Bread & Butter	2. 6.			
	Total	**£1.3.6d**		**Total**	**19. 3d**

The leftovers from these meals were served to the servants of the household, who got many a nice meal. A good cook would recycle all the food and waste nothing.

Breakfast Dishes *(Hannah Firkin)*

Chapter 4
Breakfast Recipes

9. Pigs Ears

This was also used for a main meal in the poor houses of the England in the 1800's, but was one of the most attractive dishes in the household of the gentry.

Two ears, sage and onion, quarter of suet, a handful of breadcrumbs, salt and pepper to taste, two eggs, half pint of gravy, and a piece of butter the size of a tea cup.

Parboil the ears for half an hour. Make a forcemeat of the sage, onion, finely chopped suet, breadcrumbs, pepper and salt. Mix and bind it with the beaten egg yolks. Raise the skin of the upper sides of the ears, and stuff them with it. Fry the ears in fresh butter to a nice brown. Pour away the fat and drain them. Place in the gravy and cook over the fire for half hour. Serve with fresh parsley.

10. Devilled Chicken (1811)

A cold fowl or part of one, three tablespoons of mustard, two saltspoons of salt, one teaspoonful of pepper and half a saltspoonful of cayenne pepper.

Take the wings and legs of the fowl; make incisions in them, fill these cuts with mustard. Season them highly with salt, white and cayenne pepper. Grill them over a clear fire, and serve them very dry on a hot table-napkin.

11. Devilled Chicken

There is not too much difference between the 1811 method and the method I am going to give you now for Devilled Chicken.

1 Chicken, 1 tablespoon of olive oil, salt & pepper, a pinch of ground ginger, teaspoonful of English mustard, 1 teaspoon chopped parsley, 1 teaspoon chopped shallot.

Split and skewer the chicken and sprinkle the pieces with olive oil. Season with salt and pepper, cut into the chicken and sprinkle the mustard and ginger into the cuts, and put the parsley and shallot over. Grill very slowly until tender. Serve hot with a saffron rice and cucumber salad.

12. Kippered Salmon Toasted

The Salmon, boiling water, and one ounce of butter.

Toast the salmon, place it in a basin with the outside downwards, pour boiling water over it, if salt be objected to repeat the process. Place it on a dish the right side upwards and spread butter on it before the fire. When your salmon has been poached, take out the bone and place the salmon on its side in a greased baking tray, spreading butter all over it. Sprinkle parsley, sage and chives over it and cook in the oven Gas 4 350F for ¾ hour. Serve with a warm Hollandaise or Cheese sauce.

13. Game Pie for a Hunting Breakfast (1861)

This one pie would have kept a family of six for 3 weeks in food, for breakfast, dinner and tea. What ever was left from this dish was served to the servants (probably for about three days). It would take about three and a half hours altogether to do this marvellous dish.

You would need one goose, one turkey, one snipe, two grouse, two woodcocks, one pheasant, two partridges, one and a half bullocks' tongues, the meat of one hare, one pint of good gravy, one pound of grated ham, seven pounds of flour, one and a quarter pound of suet, and two pounds of butter.

Make an ornamental crust with the flour, suet and butter, in a fancy shape, with a top to fit, and bake in a slow oven. Cut all the game and bullocks' tongue into small pieces, and stew them gently for about two hours. Put it into the crust, adding the gravy and grated ham (cooked), and a little seasoning if required. Cover with the paste top, and warm in slow oven.

All these dishes would have been decorated before being brought to the breakfast table. The game pie in 1983 would cost according to the *Caterer & Hotelkeepers 'Food Cost Index'* £72.75. In 1800 it would have cost three shillings and ninepence.

14. Game Pie

There is no way that the housewife can afford to make the Hunting Breakfast Game Pie, so I have made a little cheaper version that I am sure the average person could afford to make.

1 Pheasant, 1 partridge, ½lb cooked ham, ½lb pate, allspice, pepper, salt, gravy and a raised pie crust, glass of red wine.

Here is the recipe for a Raised Pie Crust.
10ozs plain flour, 3ozs lard, ½ teaspoon of salt and pepper mixed, ¼ pint of milk.

Sift the flour and salt, pepper into a warm bowl, make a well in the centre, and keep it in a warm place. Heat the milk and lard together until hot, then add to the flour, mixing all well with a plastic or wooden spoon, until this is cool enough to knead with your hands. Knead thoroughly for a good 5 minutes then cover with a warm damp cloth for ½ hour. Throughout this whole process the pastry must be kept warm. The pastry must be moulded while still warm. It should be rolled out to ¼ inch thick into an oval shape. Bake in a hot oven Gas 7, 425F. As soon as the pastry has set reduce to 350F, Gas 4. Do not forget to put the top in the oven separately.

Cut the birds up into small pieces, removing all the bones and place in a large saucepan with the pate, ham chopped fine, seasoning, allspice and gravy, cook slowly for 1 hour until the game is tender, add a glass of red wine if you feel it is getting too thick and dry. Put the ingredients into the pie, put on the top of the pie, ornament it, glaze with egg yolk and cook for 1½ hours in a slow oven Gas 3, 275F. With this being a very filling pie, you will find that baked parsnip and game chips would be enough to serve with this dish.

Chapter 5
The Diet of the Poor

Breakfast and the Poor Household

Breakfast for the poor was something which I have experienced by trying all of the recipes given in the next chapter and it is not food I would like to have had every day.

In the cramped and spartan conditions of the homes of the poor were no luxuries such as carpets, armchairs and beds. There was only an open fire with a homemade spit and a rude table and bench for the head of the family to sit at. The bed was a sack of straw, spread out in the same room that they ate in. The smell in these tiny houses must have been terrible. During the early years of the 19th century outbreaks of Asiatic cholera, commonly designated cholera morbus or 'Black Fever', caused many deaths throughout England; tar barrels were burnt in the public streets to disinfect the atmosphere.

In a *Chronological History of Bolton 1800* James Clegg wrote: 'Distress of the Handloom Weavers':—

> The weavers were labouring under the most incredible privation, they did not earn a sufficiency to procure them meat, except occasionally, more frequently than once a week. Their ordinary food was oatmeal and potatoes, mutton broth, gruel, mutton dripping on stale bread, water and beer. A man having a family of five children could not with the assistance of his wife and two of his children earn more than 2¾d for each, per day, applicable for food and clothing. There were 10,000 poor persons living upon 'twopence a day' in Bolton.

In 1815 Sir Robert Peel introduced in the House of Commons a Bill to deal with the labour of children. Children under nine years were not to be employed, and if you were under sixteen you could not work more than 12 hours per day. This Act, like its predecessors, was inadequately enforced and easily evaded.

The early factories were set up by the side of streams in country places, and as no accommodation existed for the workpeople, cottages were erected for them by factory owners; factory villages then came into existence. In such districts there were usually no shops other than one opened by the factory owner. The work people were then compelled to deal at that shop, where they might be encouraged to get into debt. Such debts, with the rents of their cottages, were deducted from their wages at the end of the week

19

and they might owe so much to the employer that they never became free from debt, and could not leave their employment.

In other cases they were compelled to accept payment of wages, in whole or part, in food. The payment of wages in whole or part with goods was known as *truck,* and in course of time it was prohibited under very heavy penalties by Act of Parliament. In 1887 the enforcement of the law against truck was assigned to factory inspectors.

The level of prices prevalent before the Black Fever is indicated by the fact that a halfpenny would purchase either a dozen eggs or 3 gallons of beer.

The ordinary small farmer might keep a few cows and sheep and grow mainly an oat crop. The oats were ground into meal at the local mills and used as the main food of the family. Wheaten flour was only used at times of festival and, in general, families lived on gruel and oatmeal bread.

Rather a different picture is presented when you consider purchases made by the steward for the use of the gentleman's household. Oysters were at 4 shillings per barrel, salmon at Liverpool cost £1.2/6d — a single salmon, brandy was 2 shillings a quart, wine the same price. Congo Tea was at 6s 8d per pound and Hyson Tea at 9 shillings per pound.

The poor would queue for penny pieces of bacon of which, as a girl who had purchased a penny worth commented "there is little here for six of us". Another family of 12 ate only gruel twice a day, potatoes once and herrings sometimes. The pan they used was borrowed and their clothes were pawned at night to redeem their bedding and their bedding in the morning to redeem their clothes.

Here is an extract from Charles Dickens's *Oliver Twist:*—
Poor Oliver! He little thought, as he lay sleeping in happy unconsciousness of all around him, that the board had that very day arrived at a decision which would exercise the most material influence over all his future fortunes. But they had. And this was it:

The members of this board were very sage, deep, philosophical men; and when they came to turn their attention to the workhouse, they found out at once, what ordinary folks would never have discovered — the poor people liked it! It was a regular place of public entertainment for the poorer classes; a tavern where there was nothing to pay; a public breakfast, dinner, tea and supper all the year round; a brick and mortar elysium, where it was all play and no work. "Oho!" said the board, looking very knowing; "We are the fellows to set this to rights; we'll stop it all, in no time." So, they established the rule, that all poor people should have the alternative (for they would compel nobody, not they), of being starved by a gradual process in the house, or by a quick one out of it.

TO THE

Boroughreeves and Constables

OF

GREAT AND LITTLE BOLTON,

GENTLEMEN,

We the Undersigned, request that you will call a

MEETING

On as early a Day as possible, of the LAND-OWNERS and LEY-PAYERS of Great and Little Bolton and the adjacent Townships, to take into consideration the

Distressed State

OF THE

WEAVERS,

And to co-operate with the Manufacturers in attempting to alleviate their sufferings.

John Jones,	John Dean,	J. & J. Mallett,	William West,
Peter Ormrod,	Robert Gardner,	Thomas Haslam,	John Mitchell,
W. G. Taylor,	Peter Crook,	Samuel Taylor,	Thomas Pearson,
Jonathon Hitchin,	William Taylor,	Robert Knott,	Henry Bond,
John Heaton,	Joseph Cook,	Henry Holme,	Robert Walsh,
James Haslam,	Thomas Brodbelt,	Thomas Taylor,	Wm. Moore,
Thomas Green,	Richard Kynaston,	Roger Haslam,	John Cartwright.
Charles Ainsworth,	Hugh Brodie and Co.	Richard Nightingale,	

In Compliance with the above Requisition, we hereby convene

A MEETING

Of the Land-owners and Ley-payers of Great and Little Bolton and the adjacent Townships, for the purposes above stated, to be held at the

Sessions-Room, in Great Bolton,

On FRIDAY next, the 5th MAY,

AT ELEVEN O'CLOCK IN THE FORENOON.

THOMAS BOLLING, Boroughreeve of Great Bolton
CHARLES NUTTALL, } Constables of do.
JOHN BRIMELOW,

W. G. TAYLOR, Boroughreeve of Little Bolton
JAMES COCKER, } Constables of do.
STEPHEN BLAIR,

BOLTON, 20th APRIL, 1826.

J. GARDNER, PRINTER, DEANSGATE, BOLTON.

1826 Poster *(Bolton Metropolitan Borough Council)*

21

With this view, they contracted with the water-works to lay on an unlimited supply of water; and with a corn-factor to supply periodically small quantities of oatmeal; and issued three meals of thin gruel a day, with an onion twice a week, and half a roll on Sundays.

For the first six months after Oliver Twist was removed, the system was in full operation. It was rather expensive at first, in consequence of the increase in the undertaker's bill, and the necessity of taking in the clothes of all the paupers, which fluttered loosely on their wasted, shrunken forms, after a week or two's gruel. But the number of work-house inmates got thin as well as the paupers; and the board were in ecstasies.

The room in which the boys were fed, was a large stone hall, with a copper[1] at one end, out of which the master dressed in an apron for the purpose, and assisted by one or two women, ladled the gruel at meal-times. Of this festive composition each boy had one porringer[2], and no more — except on occasions of great public rejoicing, when he had two ounces and a quarter of bread besides. The bowls never wanted washing. The boys polished them with their spoons till they shone again; and when they had performed this operation (which never took very long, the spoons being nearly as large as the bowls), they would sit staring at the copper, with such eager eyes, as if they could have devoured the very bricks of which it was composed; employing them-selves, meanwhile, in sucking their fingers most assiduously, with the view of catching up any stray splashes of gruel that might have been cast thereon.

Boys have generally excellent appetites. Oliver Twist and his companions suffered the tortures of slow starvation for three months: at last they got so voracious and wild with hunger, that one boy, who was tall for his age, and hadn't been used to that sort of thing (for his father had kept a small cook-shop) hinted darkly to his companions that unless he had another basin of gruel per diem, he was afraid he might some night happen to eat the boy who slept next to him, who happened to be a weakly youth of tender age. He had a wild, hungry eye; and they implicitly believed him. A council was held; lots were cast who should walk up to the master after supper that evening, and ask for more; and it fell to Oliver Twist.

The evening arrived; the boys took their places. The master, in his cook's uniform, stationed himself at the copper; his pauper assistants ranged themselves behind him, the gruel was served out; and a long grace was said over the short commons. The gruel disappeared, the boys whispered to each other and winked at Oliver; while his next neighbours nudged him. Child as he was, he was desperate with hunger, and reck-less with misery. He rose from the table; and advancing to the master, basin and spoon in hand, said; somewhat alarmed at his own temerity: 'Please, sir, I want some more!'

Dickens was brilliant. That was not a cry from one boy but from a world which was crying for better living conditions.

[1] A large pan.
[2] A bowl.

Chapter 6
Northern Dishes and other Recipes for the Poor

15. Mutton Broth

Three pounds of scrag of mutton, three quarts of water, two turnips, one tablespoon of pearl barley, or rice.

Boil in three quarts of water, three pounds of scrag end of neck, with two turnips sliced, and a tablespoon of pearl barley or rice. Let it boil gently for three hours, keeping it well skimmed.

16. Gruel

Two tablespoonfuls of oatmeal, half a blade of mace, three quarters of a pint of water.

Mix two spoonfuls of oatmeal very smooth in a little water, and gradually to three-quarters of a pint of water, add half a blade of mace, set it over the fire for a quarter of an hour, stirring it constantly, add sugar to taste. (If you could afford it). The wonderful thing about some of the northern recipes is the imagination and simplicity that went into them, nothing was too much trouble. For example from my book *The People of Bolton on Cookery* we have the far-famed Bury Black Pudding.

17. Bury Black Pudding

Take groats and pearl barley. Tie up loosely in a bag and boil until cooked, place in a large tub and add *seasoning, flour and onions.* Mix well whilst hot, add *back fat or leaf* cut into pieces ½ inch square, now add *blood* and stiffen with *oatmeal.* Fill into Bullock runners with a *pudding filler,* allowing about four pieces of fat for each pudding. Tie up firmly and boil gently for about 20 minutes.

That recipe is only 82 years old. But look at this recipe which was written in 1811 for *The Frugal Housewife.* Can you imagine the state the kitchen would be in after making Black Puddings.

18. Black Puddings (*The Frugal Housewife* 1811*)*

Before you kill a hog get a *peck of groats,* boil them half an hour in water, then drain them, and put them in a clean tub or large pan. Then kill your *hog,* save two quarts of the blood, and keep stirring it till it is quite cold; then mix it with your groats, and stir them well together. Season with a *large teaspoon of salt,* a *quarter of an ounce of cloves, mace, and nutmeg* together, an equal quantity of each; dry it, beat it well, and mix in.

Take a little *winter savory, sweet-marjoram, and thyme, penny-royal* stripped of the stalks and chopped very fine; just enough to season them, and to give them flavour, but no more.

The next day take the leaf of the hog, and cut it into dice, scrape, and wash the guts very clean, then tie one end, and begin to fill them, but be sure to put in a good deal of fat, fill the skins three parts full, tie the other end, and make your puddings what length you please; prick them with a pin, and put them in a kettle of boiling water. Boil them very slowly for an hour, then take them out, and lay them on clean straw.

19. Yorkshire Pudding 1811

Take *four large spoonfuls of flour,* and beat it up well with *four eggs* and *a little salt.* Then put to them *three pints of milk,* and mix them well together. Butter a dripping pan, and set it under the *beef, mutton or loin of veal.* When the meat is about half roasted, put in your pudding, and let the fat drip on it. When it is brown at top, cut into square pieces and turn it over; and when the under side is browned also, send it to table on a dish.

No matter what recipe book you look in from the first cookery book to now, it's interesting to find how different the recipe for Yorkshire pudding is. I have a vast collection of cookery books and not one recipe is the same as another.

20. Yorkshire Pudding 1868

One and a half pint of milk, seven tablespoons of flour, three eggs, and salt to taste.

Put the flour in a basin with a little salt and sufficient milk to make it into a stiff smooth batter, add the remainder of the milk and the eggs well beaten. Beat all well together, and pour into a tin that has been well buttered. Bake it for an hour, then place it under the meat for half hour to catch a little gravy that flows from the meat, cut the pudding into small squares, and serve on a napkin.

If you cut the Yorkshire pudding into little squares in Yorkshire you would not be living there very long. I have heard hundreds of different versions of how the following recipe should be served, and what it should be eaten with.

It originates from the pit workers' sandwich, it was cut into like a pocket and different fillings were put into the pudding, (why not use bread? — because it could not hold gravy!) Yorkshire pudding did hold gravy and so they could eat them down the pit. They sealed the tops after they had been filled, with another Yorkshire pudding.

It was also very filling and cheap. I have been into a miner's home and eaten Yorkshire pudding in Barnsley, I was served Yorkshire pudding before the main course, with thin gravy. It was not cut into small squares, but it was the same size as a saucer and oval. The recipe which was passed on through generations to the late Mrs Albert Frost of Barnsley, is as follows:—

21. Yorkshire Pudding Mrs A. Frost

3 heaped tablespoons of flour, 1 small teaspoon of salt, 1 egg, ½ gill milk, 1 small teaspoon of dripping, and water to the consistency of making the mixture like cream.

This recipe is enough for two persons, double the quantity as required. Put the flour into the basin and make a well in the centre. Drop in the egg, sprinkle salt round the edge of the flour, stir the egg and flour together, gradually adding milk until a stiff batter. Thin with water to the consistency of thick cream. Beat well and leave it for 1½ hours. Thoroughly heat the dripping in the tin, pour in the beaten up batter and bake in a hot oven for 20 minutes.

22. Hodge Podge (1836)

Take a pound of beef, a pound of veal and a pound of scrag of mutton.

Cut the beef into small pieces and put the whole into a saucepan, with *two quarts of water.* Take *an ounce of barley, an onion, a small bundle of sweet-herbs, three or four heads of celery washed clean and cut small, a little mace, two or three cloves and some whole pepper* tied all in a piece of cloth, and throw into the pot with the meat, *three turnips pared and cut into two, a large carrot scraped clean and cut in six pieces and a small lettuce.* Cover the pot close and let it stew very gently for five or six hours; then take out the spice, sweet herbs and onion, pour all into a soup dish, season it with salt and send it to the table.

Hodge Podge is very similar to Lancashire Hot Pot. Taken from Warnes Cookery Book 1868 the recipe for 'Hotch Potch' is *one pint of peas, 3lb lean end of a loin of mutton, 1 gal water, 4 carrots, 4 turnips, 1 onion, 1 head of celery, salt and pepper to taste.* If you take the 'ch' off the end you have Hot Pot, I wonder if there is some connection.

23. Here is my mother's recipe for Lancashire Hot Pot

2lb peeled and sliced potatoes, 1lb peeled and sliced onions, 2lb mutton chops, 1lb carrots peeled and sliced, 1 pint of good beef stock with a little dripping, salt and freshly ground pepper.

Arrange the mutton chops, onion, potatoes, carrots in layers in a casserole dish and season well with the salt and pepper, making sure the top layer is potato. Pour over the stock and dripping and put into the oven Gas 3, 325F for 2 hours, adding more stock if required to cover the casserole. Uncover ½ hour before serving to allow the top layer to get brown. Serve with fresh crusty bread.

I worked in Dublin for nearly a year in 1969 for a friend called Paul Christopher at his discotheque and restaurant called *Tiffany's.* Paul's mother Mrs Glyn would give us a big breakfast every morning of Irish ham, white pudding, potato cakes, eggs and soda bread. The Glyn family was a very big one with the smallest lad being Shay at 6 feet 13 inches without his socks on. I wanted to know what made Shay and his brothers so big. The secret was Irish Coddle. The whole art of this traditional 19th century recipe is to let the potatoes blend into the gravy and become a creamy soup. I love Ireland and the wonderful people there, if you have never been then I must say you are missing a country of true beauty.

24. Mrs Glyn's Dublin Coddle

1lb pork sausages, 1lb kidneys, 2lb lean neck of lamb chops, 2lb potatoes, 1lb of onions, sprig of thyme and parsley, 1½ pints of meat stock, salt and pepper.

Make sure the meat is trimmed of fat and gristle. Get a large saucepan and place the chops, sausage and diced kidney into the saucepan making sure you have seasoned each piece of meat. Peel and chop the onions and potatoes into 2 inch squares. Add them to the meat with the parsley, thyme and stock. Cook very slowly for 3 hours. The coddle when cooked should be thick and creamy, the potatoes having melted into the gravy. Serve with Soda Bread (see recipe number 40).

Another interesting subject is the feet of animals. The feet of animals consist of two chief chemical constituents of food, viz., oil and gelatin, and hence we have neat's foot oil and calf's foot jelly.

The oil has too strong a flavour to be used as food, and must be removed before the foot is eaten. This is affected by the application of heat after the free use of the knife, and as the foot is cooked by being boiled in water it is necessary that the oil should be skimmed from the broth that the latter may be fit for food. When properly prepared the broth contains jelly and oil, both of which may be separated and used, whilst the insoluble part of the foot contains a portion of skin and cartilage, which is nutritious and agreeable. The flavour, however, of both cow-heel and tripe is but slight, and does not stimulate the sense of taste, so that vinegar and other condiments are commonly eaten with them.

Sheeps' trotters were made into a dish in the fourteenth century with eggs, pepper, salt, saffron and raisins. Collared pork is made from the gelatinous parts of the pig, as the ears, feet and face, and was in use from the first cookery book in 1300 according to the following recipe:—

Gele of Flessh (Forme of Cury)

'Take swyn' fet and snowt' and the eerys, capons' conyin'g caln' fete, and waische he clene, and do he to seethe in the thriddel of wyne and vyneg' and wat and make forth as bifore.

25. Calfs Feet (*The Frugal Housewife* 1811)

Parboil them then take out the long bones, split them and put them into a stew pan with some *veal gravy and a glass of white wine.*

Add likewise the *yolks of two or three eggs* beat up with *a little butter.* Stir it till it is of a good thickness; and when the whole has gently simmered for about ten minutes, put the feet into your dish, and pour the sauce over them. Garnish with *sliced lemon.*

26. Tripe (*Housewifes Cookery* 1824)

Cut your tripe into pieces about two inches square, and put them into your stew pan with as much *white wine* as will cover them, *a little white pepper, sliced ginger, a blade of mace, a bunch of sweet herbs and an onion.*

When it has stewed a ¼ of an hour (which will be a sufficient time to do it), take out the herbs and onion, and put in *a little shred parsley, the juice of a lemon, half an anchovy cut small, a cupful of cream, and either the yolk of an egg, or a piece of butter.* Season it to your taste; and when you dish it up, garnish with *lemon.*

That recipe would have cost more than a turkey dinner at today's prices, only the middle of the road households could afford to do it that way. Late into the nineteenth century it was cooked this way:—

27. Tripe (*Household Cookery* 1868)

Two pounds of tripe, equal parts milk and water four large onions.

Take two pounds of fresh tripe, cleaned and dressed by the tripe-dresser, cut away the coarsest fat, and boil for 20 minutes in milk and water. Boil in the same water which boils the tripe *four large onions;* the onions should be put on the fire at least half an hour before the tripe is put into the stewpan, and then made into a rich onion sauce, which serve with the tripe. Tripe may also be cleaned, dried cut into pieces, fried in batter and served with melted butter.

I have given you two versions of nineteenth century tripe dishes, which the North of England is noted for. Here are two more modern dishes.

28. Tripe Soup (from *The People of Bolton on Cookery*)
1lb tripe, 3 pints of water, 1 turnip, 1 carrot, 3 onions, sweet herbs, parsley, ½ pint of milk, 2 tablespoons of cornflour.
First scald the tripe, and cut into very small pieces before setting to boil with cold water and herbs, chop all the vegetables into small pieces, add to the tripe and boil slowly for one hour. Then take the cornflour, work into a paste with cold milk, add to the boiling soup, and stir for ten minutes. Just before serving add remains of the milk and chopped parsley, salt and ground pepper to taste. If you want to be creative add orange juice instead of milk, with a glass of sherry and serve cold for a summer soup with garlic bread.

29. Tripe and Onions
3lb of tripe, 1lb onions, salt, pepper and vinegar.
Tripe bought at the tripe shops is already cooked and dressed, and will only require re-cooking in some suitable sauce. So boil it up again, simmer gently until tender. Drain it well, cut into convenient sized pieces for serving, and cover with a good onion sauce. Season with salt, pepper and vinegar.

30. A Lancashire Hot-pot (G.V. 1862)
This Lancashire dish is much liked; so much so, that every one at the table always partakes of it, and most persons make their dinner of it.

This dish must be made in a fireproof pan, resembling in shape a turtle-mug or cheese-pan. Cut *three pounds of rump-steak* into square pieces, cut *eight or ten potatoes* in quarters, *some whole onions, and mushrooms* if in season, all well seasoned with *cayenne, black pepper and salt,* together with *half a dozen kidneys;* place all in layers one on the other, pour over them *3 or 4 tablespoons of mushroom catchup,* and put *six or eight dozen oysters* at the top, cover it with a crust, and bake for two hours. A few *larks or snipes* are a great addition.

31. Bolton Hot-Pot *(The People of Bolton on Cookery,* Author's Grandmother, 1880's)
1lb lean beef, 1½lb of sliced potatoes, ¾lb bacon, 1 onion, salt and pepper, ¼ pint of beef stock.
Cut the meat into ½ inch pieces, cut onion into thin slices. Put a layer of potatoes at the bottom of an earthenware dish, then a layer of meat, add a few slices of onion, and season with salt and pepper. Continue until all the ingredients are used up, potato forming the top layer. Fill the dish with the beef stock, adding more if the dish appears dry. Top with slices of bacon, cover with greased paper and bake slowly for 2 hours.

There are plenty more versions to this famous Lancashire dish, recipes which I am sure are all as good as the one above. And the following day you may add what has been left of the vegetable, and any little jelly or gravy you may have in the larder, which, with a little pepper, will make a delicious potage. A turbot, dressed as you would cook a turtle, will make a soup which is preferred by many to turtle soup.

Toad in the Hole
This is another one of those recipes that you hear the old wives' tales about. Over two hundred years ago was told the fairy story of Diamonds or Toads? — which is it to be, girls, diamonds or toads! — in which the good girl is endowed with the faculty of scattering diamonds and pearls around her, while the unsatisfactory girl is condemned to distribute toads in the same fashion. Now, which will you choose? Why make a choice, some matter of fact little maiden remarks, for fairy stories are not true. The word in this issue is cheapness (toad).

The hole is the dish in which the cheap meat is used. Mrs Beeton used 1½lbs of rump steak and a sheep's kidney in her recipe book in 1861. In 1868 Mary Jewry wrote for her recipe *take 1 chicken, veal stuffing.* Yet my grandmother's recipe is sausage. In a modern cookery book I have read 'Toad in the Hole, use chuck steak'. It is too obvious that this was a poor man's meal. And here are the three versions which I have modernised for you.

32. Toad-in-the-Hole Mrs Beeton 1861
1lb of rump steak, 1 sheep's kidney diced, ½pint of pancake batter made with milk.
Fry the diced steak and kidney for 10 minutes in butter. Place them in a roasting tin and into a preheated oven, at 425f (mark 7), for a further 10 minutes. Remove the tin from the oven. Cook for about 30 minutes, until the batter is well-risen, and after pour the batter over the meat.

33. Toad-in-the-Hole Mary Jewry 1868
A chicken, some veal stuffing, 3 eggs, 1 pint of milk, some flour.
Draw, bone and truss a chicken, fill it with a veal stuffing. Making a batter with a pint of milk, 3 eggs, and sufficient flour to make it thick, pour it deep into a buttered dish. Place the fowl in the centre of the batter, and bake in the oven as above. Use the same recipe as above to employ the modern version.

34. Toad-in-the-Hole Jessie Tong (author's grandmother)
This is the more well known method for a lot of people. It is the traditional British dish.
1lb of pork sausages and ¾ pint of Yorkshire pudding batter which you will find on page 25.
Grease a roasting tin with a teaspoon of dripping, and place the sausage into it. Place the tin in a pre-heated oven, at Gas 7, 425F, for 12 minutes. Remove the tin from the oven, and pour the batter over the sausages, and return to the oven. Cook for about 35-40 minutes. Serve with boiled potatoes and fresh mint peas with a thin gravy.

35. Bubble and Squeak
Bubble and squeak, a fry up, was a favourite during the eighteenth century, nineteenth century and today's twentieth century. The earliest use of the term so far discovered was in *A Burlesque Translation of Homer* written by my namesake Thomas Bridges in 1767.

> We therefore cook'd him up a dish
> of lean bull-beef with cabbage fried,
> and a full pot of beer beside:
> Bubble they call this dish, and squeak;
> Our taylors dine on't thrice a week.

36. Bubble and Squeak

Potatoes and Cabbage fried with beef pieces fried separately was the next form at the beginning of the 19th century.

We need a pan that's lined with grease
to put the cabbage chopped,
Then line with onions and mash spuds
and mix together the lot,
When frying lightly on the stove
To this thy seasoning add,
And with this dish,
You serve good beef,
And Bubble and Squeak you've had.

Author in 1983

Chapter 7
Public Health

In no other respect do conditions of life at the present day contrast more sharply with those of time past than in the health of the people. So much attention is paid today to living under hygienic conditions, so marked is the progress of medical science, so vigorous is the supervision maintained by the State and by local authorities over matters affecting the health of the community, that it is now possible to look forward to the time when all diseases will be regarded as not only curable but preventible, and when apart from accident, the only normal cause of death will be old age.

That desirable time may be distant yet. In the early nineteenth century man had no knowledge of elementary hygienic rules, medical science was in its infancy, and no serious effort was made by the authorities, local or national, to remedy conditions prejudicial to health.

There was no proper water-supply and no adequate system of sanitation, in town or country. Disease of all kinds was prevalent — so much so that sudden death from infectious disease was even more feared than shortage of food, itself not a remote contingency. The essentials of improvement were twofold — the provision of an adequate water supply and the establishment of main drainage. An epidemic of cholera appeared in 1847 – 8, and public opinion was aroused to a realisation of the necessity for action. In 1848 a central Board of Health was established, and it was empowered to set up a local Board of Health "in the city, town, borough, parish or village" which wished for it or in which the death rate was high. The duties of these local authorities included the provision of a supply of water, and the cleaning of streets. By 1875 the Public Health Act of that year required each sanitary authority to appoint a medical officer of health, a surveyor, and a sanitary inspector. It was expected to deal with "nuisances" wherever they arose, and it was authorised to seize and destroy unsound food.

Chapter 8
Bread

One of the most important events of the reign of Victoria was the repeal of the Corn Laws. High duties had been charged on all corn brought into the country from abroad. This made bread dear; and Richard Cobden proposed that the duties should be taken off. The farmers went against this with all their might, as they wished to get a high price for their corn. They called loudly for 'Protection' but by the eloquent speeches of Mr Cobden and Sir Robert Peel, the cause of "Free Trade" triumphed and the duty on wheat was done away with.

37. Corn Meal Pudding 1846
Two quarts of water, one tablespoon of salt, some corn meal.
Mix the ingredients in a batter as thick as you can stir easily, or until the stick will stand in it, stir it a little longer, let the fire be gentle, and when it is sufficiently done it will bubble or puff up. Then turn it into a deep dish, and eat it hot or cold, with milk or with butter and syrup or sugar, or with meat and gravy, the same as potatoes or rice.

This recipe was made just after the corn laws were repealed. Considering there were to be improvements in food this was to be a poor substitute for potatoes or rice. I would stick to rice. Bread was made from Indian Corn Flour from the 1840's to late into the 1860's because it was cheaper than our home-grown produce.

38. Indian Corn Flour Bread 1840

Half a stone of Indian corn, one stone of fine wheaten flour, a ¼ lb of salt, 4 quarts of boiling water, 2 quarts of yeast.

Take half a stone of Indian corn, pour upon it four quarts of boiling water, stirring it all the time. Let it stand till it is about new milk warm, then mix with it a stone of fine wheaten flour, to which a ¼ lb of salt has previously been added. Make a hollow in this mixture and pour into it 2 quarts of yeast, previously thickened to the consistence of cream by the mixture of a little flour. Let it stand all night. On the following morning the whole should be well kneaded and allowed to stand for 3 hours. Then divide it into loaves, which are better baked in tins, in which they should stand for ½ an hour, then bake them.

Result? 32 pounds of wholesome, nutritive, and very agreeable bread. The recipe might be over 143 years old, but very hard to beat in today's value of wheatgerm.

39. Author's Corn Bread

Now try my recipe. For a special flavour use bacon dripping to grease your baking tin instead of shortening.

1 cup of corn meal, 1 cup of flour, 1 tablespoon sugar, 4 teaspoons baking powder, 1 teaspoon salt, ⅛ teaspoon of ground white pepper, 1 egg, 1 cup of milk, ¼ cup of vegetable shortening, 1½ tablespoons of bacon drippings.

Sift the dry ingredients together into a large mixing bowl, add the egg, milk and ¼ cup of shortening, and beat with a wooden spoon until smooth, about 2 minutes. Grease an 8 to 10 inch baking tin with the bacon fat, pour in the batter and bake in a preheated oven Gas 7, 425F for 25 to 30 minutes until golden brown.

40. Irish Soda Bread

1lb of wholewheat flour, ½lb plain flour, 1 teaspoon bicarbonate of soda, ½ pint of buttermilk and a teaspoon salt.

Mix together the flour, soda and salt, make a well in the centre. Add milk to make a thick dough and stir with a spatula. The dough should be slack but not wet. Mix the dough lightly, adding a little extra milk if it seems to be firm. Flatten the dough on a floured board, make a circle about 2 inches thick. Put it onto a baking sheet, and mark a large cross with a knife. Bake in a hot oven Gas 6, 400F or 200C for 40 minutes. Let the bread go cold for about 5 hours before cutting.

THE MYSTERIE AND TRADE OF BAKING

All services that to the Baker's Trade
Or mysterie belong, be here displaid,

Which my rude Arts in order shall recount,
And those in number to thirteen amount,
Being (how ere such Tradesmen used to coozen
In their scale measure) just a Baker's dozen.

First ¹Boulting, ²Seasoning, ³Casting up, and ⁴Braking,
⁵Breaking out dowe, next ⁶Weighing, or weight making
(Which last is rarely seene), then some doe ⁷Mould;
This ⁸Cuts, that ⁹Seales and Sets up, yet behold
The seasoner ¹⁰Heating, or with Barin fires
Preparing the oven as the case requires;

2a

The Mysterie and Trade of Baking (*The Ma*

36

One carrying up, the Heeter peeleth on
And playes the [11] Setter, who's no sooner gone
But the hot mouth is [12] Stopt, so to remaine
Untill the setter [13] drawes all forth againe.

Thus bakers make and to perfection bring,
No less to serve the Beggar than the King,
All sorts of Bread, which being handled well,
All other food and Cates doth farre excell.
Let Butchers, Poultrers, Fishmongers contend
Each in his own trade, in what he can Defend,
Though Flesh, Fish, Whitemeat, all in fitting season,
Nourish the body, being used with reason,
Yet no man can deny (to end the strife)
Bread is worth all, being the staff of life.

r and Confectioner — Kirkland)

37

Chapter 9
The Victorian Lunch

"LUNCH" modern abbreviation of 'luncheon' was in its original form "LUNCHIN" nothing but a big slice or lump of bread or other eatable. This would be particularly applicable to the big lump of bread or cheese off which a labourer still makes his midday meal. Gay in 1714, wrote, "I sliced the luncheon from the barley-loaf". The sense of the word was in course of time easily extended to that of the light meal we now eat at noon. Thus the original sense of luncheon was a noonday slice or lump of bread or cheese. It may be worthwhile mentioning here that the now familiar 'Sandwich' which is part of all picnics and outings, and the long distance lorry driver's friend, gets its name from the fourth Earl of Sandwich who, being a confirmed gambler, invented it in order to remain at the gaming table without interruption (I don't think the saying, 'Put your money where your mouth is', came from the Earl).

Lunch was simple, with chops, hashes, pasties, cold pork pie, cheese with raw onion. Cold joints of lamb, beef and venison were ever so popular. They would drink wine, claret and champagne and cider cups were favourites in summer. The normal working family would live off cheese or herrings with rough bread, stout or water, if they could afford it. At twopence a day it was very expensive to have lunch.

Chapter 10
Pies and Pasties

Here are two of those delightful summer luncheon recipes.

41. Cheshire Pork Pie *The Frugal Housewife* 1811
Take *the skin of a loin of pork, and cut it into steaks.* Season them with *pepper, salt, and nutmeg,* and make a good crust. Put into your dish a layer of pork, then a layer of *pippins,* pared and cored, and *sugar* sufficient to sweeten it. Then place another layer of pork, and put in half a pint of *white wine* . Lay some *butter* on the top, close your pie, and send it to the oven. If your pie is large, you must put in a pint of white wine.

42. Cheshire Pork Pie
There are several versions of this famous pie. This one is from The Royal George of Knutsford where I worked as freelance Head Chef for Carne's Catering Agency in Manchester. The Royal George is a well known eating establishment.
2lbs of Pork, 3ozs butter, 6 Cox's pippins, 2ozs sugar, salt, pepper and nutmeg, a glass of white wine. Raised pie crust as above.
Cut the pork into thin steaks flattened out, season them with the salt, pepper and nutmeg. Put your layer of pork in the pie, peel and core the apples and slice thinly. Then alternatively layer apple and pork until all is used up, pour in the wine mixed with the sugar and a little gravy, cover with ½oz butter, put your lid on the pie and egg it once, and bake for 1½ hours Gas 3, 275F.

43. Venison Pasty *Young Womans Companion* 1811
Take *a neck and breast of venison* bone them, and season them well with *salt and pepper,* put them into a deep pan, with the best part of *the neck of mutton* sliced and laid over them; pour in *a glass of red wine,* put a *coarse paste* over it, and put *one pound of butter* over it; make a *good puff paste,* and lay it near half inch thick round the edge of a dish, and lay it on, then roll out another lid pretty thin, and cut in flowers, leaves or whatever you please, and lay it on the lid. If you do not want it, it will keep in the pot that it was baked in eight to ten days; but let the crust be kept on, that the air may not get to it. A breast and shoulder of venison is the most proper for a pasty.

44. Venison Pasty

The translated version from the *Young Womans Companion* would be Venison Pie with the old fashioned raised crust. Take *the neck of venison* and remove the bones and skin and cut the meat into ½ inch squares. Put them into a large saucepan with a *large chopped onion, a good stock either veal or chicken, salt and pepper to taste.* Add *a glass of red wine* and *a small glass of port* and cook for 2 hours until tender. Take out the venison and make a roux adding the stock that is over from the venison. Cook out the sauce for 10 minutes then put the venison into the pie, add the sauce, put on the crust and bake in the oven Gas 3, 325F for 1 hour. Serve with new potatoes and spring cabbage (fried).

45. Hare Pie (1811)

Cut your *hare* into pieces, and season it well with *pepper, salt, nutmeg and mace.* Then put it into a jug with *half a pound of butter,* close it up, set it in a copper of boiling water and make a rich forcemeat with *a quarter of a pound of scraped bacon, two onions, a glass of red wine, the crumb of a penny loaf, a little winter savoury, the liver cut small, and a little nutmeg.* Season it high with *pepper and salt;* mix it well up with *the yolks of three eggs,* raise the pie and lay the forcemeat in the bottom of the dish. Then put in the hare, with the gravy that came out of it; lay on the lid and send it to the oven. An hour and a half will bake it.

46. Herring Pie (1811)

Having scaled, gutted and washed your *herrings* clean, cut off their heads, fins and tails. Make a good crust, cover your dish and season your herrings with *beaten mace, pepper and salt.* Put *a little butter* in the bottom of your dish and then the herrings. Over these put *some apples and onions* sliced very thin. Put some butter on the top, then pour in a little water, lay on the lid, send it to the oven and let it be well baked.

These recipes are done the same today as they were then, both would be put in the oven at Gas 5 375F for ¾ to 1 hour.

47. Beefsteak & Oyster Pie (Author's recipe)

2lb Fillet Steak, 2 dozen Oysters, ½lb Puff Pastry, white stock, cayenne, ½ glass of rosé wine, salt and freshly ground white pepper.

Cut the fillet steak into thin slices, flatten them out, then wrap up an oyster in each slice. Place each layer dusted with salt, ground pepper and cayenne into a pie dish, mix the wine with the white stock then pour over the steak and oysters until it is just covered. Roll out the puff pastry to a quarter of an inch thick, cover the dish and with the trimmings make leaves and decorate, egg wash and place the pie dish in a baking tray of boiling water and bake in a moderate oven for 35 minutes or until golden brown.

Serve with baked onions in white sauce to complement the pie.

Chapter 11
The Victorian Tea

High teas were served at the large afternoon gatherings where the elite would gossip, I cannot think of a better word because that is all it was, 'tattle' is the phrase the English dictionary uses.

Imagine a large drawing room with 14 ladies chatting away, "I went to St James's Theatre on Saturday to see the new play, *Lady Windermere's Fan* by Oscar Wilde". "Yes he's coming to tea next week!"

There would be music playing, and they would talk about who was doing what, with who and when. It was a permanent institution in most Victorian houses to have a high tea. At the usual high tea there are probably to be found one or two small hot dishes, cold chickens or game, tongue or ham, salad, cakes of various kinds, cold fruit tarts with cream or custard and fresh fruit.

High Tea *(Hannah Firmin)*

Chapter 12
Tea Recipes

Here are some lovely recipes that they would have had at high tea. I have modernised all these recipes to make sure that you too can use them at a modern tea.

48. Smoked Salmon Pâté
½lb of flaked smoked salmon, 3ozs soured cream, 8oz carton of cottage cream cheese, (sieved), ½oz butter melted, grated rind and juice of ½ lemon, salt and pepper.
Place the salmon in a blender, add the cream and cheese and blend until smooth. Stir in the butter, lemon rind and juice, salt and pepper to taste. Turn into small dishes, chill and serve with brown bread.

49. Chicken & Mushroom Patties
6ozs chopped cooked chicken, 3ozs cooked and chopped mushrooms, a pinch of crushed rosemary, 1oz butter, 2 tablespoons of flour, 6 tablespoons of stock, salt and pepper, also 8ozs puff pastry (which I have already given you on page 18), *1 egg, 3 tablespoons of milk.*
Combine the chicken, mushroom and rosemary. Melt the butter in a saucepan and stir in the flour. Cook gently for 3 minutes, gradually add the stock and season to taste. Cook for 4 minutes and stir in the milk, remove from the heat and beat in the egg. Stir in the chicken mixture, leave to go cold.

Roll out the pastry and cut out 8 circles. Use half of these to line a Yorkshire pudding tin or little cake tins. Fill with the chicken mixture and cover with the remaining pastry rounds. Trim the edges, moisten and seal. Prick the tops, brush with beaten egg and bake in a hot oven Gas 7, 425F for 25 minutes.

50. Cream Scones

To ½lb flour allow a teaspoonful of baking powder, 2ozs butter, ¼ pint of cream, ¼ pint of milk and a pinch of salt.

Sieve together the salt, baking powder and flour, then rub in the butter. Add the cream, stir it well, then add the milk and blend into a dough. Turn out on to a floured pastry-board.

It is important for the success of these scones rising, not to use a rolling pin or pastry cutter, they only take out the air, that will make the scones light and fluffy. Press the mixture down to ½ inch thick and cut into triangles with a very sharp knife. Have a floured baking sheet ready to place them on, brush them over with egg, place them in a hot oven Gas 7 for 15 minutes. They will be very light and are lovely with jam or fresh cream.

51. Angels on Horseback

A very popular dish for high teas and cocktail parties during Victorian meetings for the upper class.

12 oysters, 12 small croûtes of fried bread, 12 thin rashers of bacon (rindless), cayenne pepper and a little parsley.

Take off the beards from the oysters and season them with a little cayenne. Encase each oyster in a strip of bacon. Put them on skewers, and set them in a baking tray. Put them in a hot oven and cook for 10 minutes. Drain well, then fry the croûtes of bread in a little butter, place one oyster and bacon on each croûte. Place a sprig of parsley on each and serve hot.

52. Scotch Shortbread

10ozs butter, 6ozs castor sugar, 1lb flour, 2 eggs, 3 drops vanilla.

Sieve the flour and make a well in the centre. Cream the sugar and eggs in the centre, add the butter and cream them together, add the vanilla, then work the mixture into the flour.

Scrape the paste down 2 or 3 times with a pallet knife until it is clear. The paste becomes oily if cleared by hand because of the heat from the hands. Place in a refrigerator to set, then roll it out ½ inch thick. Cut the paste into fancy shapes, brush them with egg wash, dredge with castor sugar and decorate with cherries and bake in the oven at 375F for 20 minutes.

53. Coconut Macaroons

Another great favourite, which I myself like very much. Prince Albert always had these dainties on hand (coconut was a very popular fruit and rare in this period).

1 dessertspoonful of flour, ¼lb desiccated coconut, ¼lb castor sugar, the whites of 2 eggs, a pinch of salt and rice paper.

Sieve the flour and sugar and mix in the coconut. Whip the whites of the eggs to a stiff peak, put in the pinch of salt, and stir them into the dry ingredients. On squares of rice paper form small heaps, and bake in a slow oven until the macaroons are firm and a pale brown colour. When they are cool trim off the edges of rice paper. Sprinkle a little castor sugar over and let them cool a little more.

Chapter 13
Food in Institutions

Food in Schools

Dotheboys Hall, the school created by Charles Dickens, was no exaggeration of the conditions of the 19th century:—

> Into these bowls, Mrs. Squeers . . . poured a brown composition, which looked like diluted pin-cushions without the covers, and was called porridge. A minute wedge of brown bread was inserted into each bowl. At one o'clock the boys having previously had their appetites thoroughly taken away by stirabout and potatoes, sat down in the kitchen to some hard salt beef. *(Nicholas Nickleby 1839).*

The diet was very bad even in the more expensive schools. Here is a typical day:— Rise at 5.30 am and do preparation until 8.00 am when they would have breakfast of gruel, bread and tea with syrup, until 8.30 am. Preparation would then carry on until 1.30 pm. 1.30 pm to 2.00 pm they would toilet and change their books for the next period. 2.00 pm dinner would follow, consisting of boiled meat or fish with potatoes, with rice pudding or a suet pudding.

2.30 pm until 5.30 pm more schooling, then they would have bread with dripping, tea, or cheese and bread. Study in their rooms until 8.00 pm

Is it any wonder that they had scurvy and lice and were weak and pale in the 1830s.

Workhouses and Prisons

The workhouse and prison food was not that tasty, with ½lb bread with gruel for breakfast, and bread and soup for lunch. The soup would have been made with ox-heads, with other meat, in the proportion of 1 ox-head for about 120 people. This would be repeated for the evening meal without the bread. In view of the deaths this diet caused, in 1835 there was appointed a Committee of the House of Lords, which did nothing until Sir James Graham devised a prison diet in 1843. This was a mere slight improvement. He added milk to the soup with bits of meat and potatoes, so instead of slops they got slops with milk and potatoes. And in the evenings they got cocoa, if they had been sentenced to more than 4 months hard labour (I can see all the little Fagins queuing to get in!).

Oscar Wilde's prison diet was mostly gruel according to *The Morning* newspaper of 6th June 1895; so called stir-about made of coarse Indian meal-suet, water, and greasy cocoa, was a frequent cause of diarrhoea, he would exercise for an hour after breakfast, then return to his cell, dinner would consist of greasy bacon and beans or soup and one day a week he would have meat.

From *The Ballad of Reading Gaol* by Oscar Wilde:—

And alien tears will fill for him
    Pity's long broken urn
For his mourners will be outcast men
    And outcasts always mourn

Chapter 14
Canapés

The Victorian hostess knew that although the man of the house might be a good mixer she must exercise some ingenuity regarding the preparation and choice of foods. A critical connoisseur of food at an informal party would be charmed and satisfied if served with well made and appetising food.

Success has been found when the food is varied but also easy to eat. For example canapés may be varied not only by their filling but also their base. They may be made of toasted bread, crisp rounds or strips of bread, pastry rounds, cheese pastry, biscuits or fried bread. When being served at cocktail parties they are generally cold.

54. Canapés — Bases
Some canapés of a simple angular shape can be prepared just as they were at the parties in Victorian gatherings. *A whole strip of bread* which had been buttered and cut from a rectangular white or brown loaf is placed on a cutting board. It is then covered along its whole length with *a topping* prepared according to any recipe which lends itself to this procedure. The topping is pressed down with a pallet knife and the bread is then cut carefully into canapés (square, triangular, oblong or diamond shapes).

For preference they should be so small that they are comparatively one mouthful. The fillings can be varied and sometimes these are spread flat, sometimes heaped and with others the bread or pastry is scooped out to form a cradle for the filling. Decorative garnishes are also added, pieces of pineapple, olives, tomato, egg; any garnish that does not clash with the colour of the filling.

55. Toast
Cut the *bread* ¼ inch thick, toast evenly on both sides, cut off the crust (which should be blended and used in your other fillings) then cut into your desired shape, this is more economical than stamping the toast into round shapes, although sometimes this is done. As a rule toast canapés are spread with a savoury butter and then decorated.

56. Bread
Cut the slices of *bread* ¼ inch thick and with a pastry cutter 2 inch in diameter stamp into rounds. Fancy shapes may be cut as well as plain rounds, provided they are the same 2 inches in diameter. If preferred, the bread may be cut into strips about 2½ inches long and 1½ inches wide. These strips will be found very convenient, as when the canapés compound is spread on, one end can be left unspread, and then can be handled and eaten without soiling the fingers. These rounds or shapes are now fried golden brown in butter, drained on white napkins and left to go cold.

57. Pastry Bases
This is the original Victorian method which was made of *ordinary short pastry,* but what is termd *rough puff pastry* is better still, particularly if the canapés resemble minature vol-au-vents, which is always a favourite snack at parties. Cheese pastry too, cut into rounds or fancy shapes makes an admirable base.

Here is the Cheese pastry base from a (modernised) Mrs Beeton's recipe.

58. Cheese Pastry Base (1861)
Allow to *½ lb self-raising flour ½ teaspoonful salt and a pinch of cayenne, 3 ozs of grated cheese, ¼ lb butter, yolk of 1 egg, a dessertspoonful of cold water* to which *a squeeze of lemon juice* is added.
Sieve the flour, salt and cayenne into a mixing bowl. Rub in the butter as for short pastry, then add the grated cheese and mix well together. Mix to a stiff paste with the yolk of an egg, lemon juice, and water. Bind together and roll out ¼ inch thick, then cut into rounds or strips, lay lightly on a floured baking sheet and bake for 15 minutes regular mark 4 or 375F.

Chapter 15
Dinner in the Victorian Household

Dinner, being the grand solid meal of the day, is a matter of considerable importance; and "a well-served table is a striking index of human ingenuity and resource" said Mrs Beeton in her *All about Cookery*. She went on to say:—

> The elegance with which a dinner is served depends, of course, partly upon the means, but still more upon the taste of the master and mistress of the house. It may be observed in general, that there should always be flowers on the table, and, as they form no item of expense where a garden is, there is no reason why they should not be employed every day.
>
> The variety of the dishes which furnish forth a modern dinner-table does not necessarily imply anything unwholesome or anything capricious. Food that is not well relished cannot be well digested; and the appetite of the overworked man of business, or statesman, or of any dweller in towns, whose occupations are exciting and exhausting must suit their mode of dining to their mode of living.

If that applied today the dinners would be very small.

Food was always a grand occasion when it came to the dinner in the households of the rich. Prince Regent would spend hundreds of pounds wining and dining at Brighton, Oscar Wilde would eat and drink all night at The Café Royal, entertaining Max Beerbohm, Bosey, Whistler and many more of his eccentric friends before going on to *Kettners* to drink even more wine, money being no object. A typical menu for the Victorian dinner would be.

	Upper Class Menu
Soup	Caviare
Whitebait Fried	Game Soup
Veal Cutlets	Filleted Soles
Roast Turkey	Lobster Cream
Lobster Salad	Curried Prawns
Sirloin of Beef	Rump Steak and Oyster Sauce
Greengage Tart and Custard	Fried Potatoes
Compote of Peaches	Vanilla Souffle
	Cost £8.15s.

For a party of ten that would cost less than £3.00 in 1865.

Chapter 16
Soups

59. Julienne Soup G.V. 1862

Julienne soup is made of *carrots, turnips, leeks, onion, celery, lettuce, sorrel, chervil, parsnips, haricots and bruised peas.* Chopped up fine together. Put 2ozs of butter into a saucepan; when it begins to melt, add a spoonful of flour, and an onion chopped very fine; stir together until it becomes quite red. You then put in the vegetables; place the saucepan on your cooker and let them simmer for an hour, stirring them often to prevent burning, and when they become lightly brown, put in 2 pints of veal broth; let it boil, and skim the top for any dirt, afterwards add a *bouquet of thyme, bay-leaves, garlic, and parsley* tied up together, and put them in the soup. Cook for a further hour and then add a *puree of peas (mushy peas) half a spoonful of brown suguar, a little salt and pepper to taste.*

From G.V's book *Dinners & Dinner Parties* 1862:—

Thick soups are not to be tolerated; it is very well to give those kind of soups to cricketers, boat rowers, and the like, but it is not allowable to choke your guests off their dinner. If soup be desirable, let it be as the French have it — a potage; and if it should happen that early in the season you should indulge in green peas or asparagus, do as the French do — boil them not in too much water, and only a little salt; save the water in which they have been boiled.

I completely disagree with G.V. I was brought up on thick homely soups and in Victorian England the poor lived on mostly broths and thick soups that would be a main course. Here are a few examples of Victorian thick soup and the broths I am myself a great lover of.

60. Mock Turtle Soup 1811

Ten pounds of the shin of beef, a bunch of sweet herbs, 2 onions, half a calf's head, a very little flour, a little pounded mace and cloves, two spoonfuls of mushroom ketchup, salt and pepper, and suet dumplings.

Take about 10 lb of shin and cut into cubed slices, and fry it off until brown, then put it into a stewpan with boiling water for eight hours with a bunch of sweet herbs and 2 onions. When cold take off the fat. Then get half a calf's head with the skin on, half boil it, and cut it into small square pieces, put it into the soup, and let it stew all together till quite tender. Thicken it with very little flour, add the mace, cloves, mushroom ketchup, and *a little soy*. Season it with salt and pepper to your taste. Put in the suet dumplings (dough ball), and a *wine glass of sherry*.

"Soup of the evening, beautiful soup!" sings the Mock Turtle in *Alice in Wonderland*. Revised version; cut the shin down to 2lb, adding *tomato puree* instead of mushroom ketchup, and *the stalks of mushrooms sliced,* also *using 1lb of beef stock* and cook for 2 hours not 10.

Soup recipes for which Stock is necessary:—

61. Consomme Julienne

1½ pints of clear brown stock, 1 carrot, 1 small turnip, 1 stick of celery.

Shred the carrot and turnip and cut the celery very finely into strips, then add to the stock. Bring to the boil and simmer gently for 10 minutes. Remove scum as it rises with a spoon.

62. Consomme Au Ritz

1½ pints of clear beef stock, 1 oz rice, 1 pint of water. Boil the rice in a pint of water till soft, strain wash off, add to the stock and boil. Add *a half glass of sherry, with salt and freshly ground pepper to taste.*

63. Consomme Royal

½ pint of clear stock, 1 egg, 1 glass of port, salt and pepper.

Beat up the egg with the ½ pint of clear stock, put in a well greased basin over slowly boiling water till it is firm, but on no account let it boil. Allow it to cool. Turn it on to a plate and cut into fancy shapes. Place them in a hot tureen and pour hot consomme over. Serve at once.

64. Cock-a-leekie

An old fowl, 5 large leeks, 2 onions, 2ozs pearl barley (soaked overnight), salt and pepper to taste.

Boil an old fowl with the onions for 2½ hours, then strain it and take off the grease. Wash the leeks, take off any coarse green leaves, and cut into inch lengths. Put the stock in a saucepan, add the pearl barley, bring it to the boil and simmer gently for an hour, putting in the leeks for the last ¼.

Cut the best bits of meat off the fowl and cut them into fairly large pieces. Put them into the stock with the salt and pepper and reheat without bringing it to the boil.

65. Cornmeal Dumplings for Soups 1844 (modernised)

Mix *a teacupful of corn meal with 2ozs of plain flour, 1oz suet, salt and pepper to taste,* mix all together and make into a dough with 4 tablespoons of water, shape into small balls, roll them in flour, and cook for 10 minutes in the boiling soup.

66. Potato Dumplings 1874 (modernised)

Boil *4 medium potatoes,* mash them with *a little butter and half beaten egg.* Season with *salt and pepper,* then beat well in *2ozs flour* and *1oz semolina.* Add a little *milk* if it seems too dry, but you are aiming at a stiff paste. Shape into small balls and cook them in boiling salted water for 15 minutes then add to your soup.

67. Oxtail Soup 1865 (modernised)

1 oxtail, 2 pints of good beef stock, 1 carrot sliced, 1 turnip sliced, 3 bay leaves, 1 teaspoon of mixed herbs, 6 peppercorns, 3 cloves ¼ teaspoon of celery salt and 1 dessertspoonful of cornflour.

Wash the tail well, wipe, break up into pieces and put into a saucepan with enough butter to prevent burning. Shake it about until it is brown. Then add the stock, vegetables, celery salt, and the bay leaves, peppercorns, cloves and herbs tied up in a muslin bag. Simmer gently for about 2½ hours, season and strain, putting back the smaller pieces of the tail.

Reheat and thicken with a little cornflour made into a paste with milk, adding a little gravy browning if necessary.

68. French Beef Soup (Camp Fashion) *Alexis Soyer* (1855)
(Adapted by the author)
Put into a large pan *2lbs of beef,* cut into three pieces, bone
included; *1lb of mixed green vegetables, 1 teaspoonful of salt,* if
handy *½ teaspoon of pepper, one of sugar and a clove, two pints
of water,* let it boil gently for 3 hours; remove some of the fat and
serve. The addition of a pound of *bread or broken biscuits,* well
soaked, will make a very nutritious soup.

69. Calfs Head Soup 1833
Wash the *head* as clean as possible, which you will the more easily
do by strewing a *little salt* on it to take out the slime. After it is
thoroughly cleansed, put it into your stewpan, with a proper
quantity of water, and throw in a *bunch of sweet herbs, an onion
stuck with cloves, five blades of mace, and some pearl barley.*
When it has stewed till it is tender, put in *some stewed celery.*
Season it with *pepper,* pour the soup into your dish, place the head
in the middle, and serve it to the table.

To try and get hold of a calf's head today is more difficult than
making the soup.

In a scene in Shakespeare's *Henry V,* the swaggering Pistol,
having threatened to make Fluellen, that is, Llewellyn, eat the leek
(the honourable badge assumed by certain brave Welshmen, who
"did good service in a garden where leeks did grow") has the tables
turned upon him, and is forced to eat it himself.

Nevertheless the leek, so long recognised as the Welshman's
emblem, was once his favourite food, and when, by ancient
custom, the Welsh farmers met to help in ploughing each other's
land, each brought a leek for the common meal.

Vichyssoise which is commonly known as leek and potato soup is
supposedly to come from France, which I do not believe for one
minute, and I am sure is an original Welsh recipe that the French
took the credit for. I always serve it chilled.

70. Leek & Potato Soup

2lb leeks, 1lb potatoes, 2 sticks of celery, 2ozs best butter, ¾ pint of milk, ½ pint of double cream, salt and ground black pepper.

Wash the leeks and take off any coarse outer leaves and trim the roots. Slice the leeks diagonally into ¼ inch pieces. Peel and dice the potatoes ½ inch in diameter. Melt the butter in a large saute or frying pan and add the potato and leeks. Cook slowly for 5 minutes, while this is cooking, wash and chop very fine the celery and add to the pan with the milk and stock, bring to the boil and season with salt and freshly ground black pepper. Simmer for 30 minutes. Allow the soup to cool slightly before putting through a very fine sieve or liquidising and test it for the right amount of seasoning. Stir in the cream and chill the soup in a refrigerator for at least 3 hours before service. Garnish with *finely chopped parsley and grated carrot.* A wonderful summer starter for an outside barbecue.

Chapter 17
The Victorian Supper

Supper was not what we have today, a cup of drinking chocolate and a few chocolate biscuits. Supper dances and supper receptions were the fashion of the Victorian night life. The Ball supper would consist of a Salmon Mayonnnaise, Lobster Patties, Chicken, Tongue, Pigeon Pie, Lamb Salads of two kinds, Galantine of Veal, Foie Gras Sandwiches, Cucumber Sandwiches, Trifles, Cream Jellies, Fancy Cakes with an assortment of fruit. A family supper would be Cold lamb with mint sauce, stewed fruit of some sort followed by cheese and biscuits.

Here is a typical week's menu for a middle class family:—

Sunday: Cold roast beef, beetroot, any cold sweet, Macaroni cheese, biscuits and butter.

Monday: Curry of cold meat or poultry, tongue. Stewed Prunes and rice, cheese and biscuits.

Tuesday: Hashed turkey, cold fish, pickles. Cold pudding, cheese and biscuits.

Wednesday: Kidney Toast, cold meat, chutney, baked rice pudding, cheese and biscuits.

Thursday: Salmi of game, brawn and beetroot, jam tartlets, cheese and biscuits.

Friday: Mayonnaise of cold fish, cake, Welsh rarebit, biscuits.

Saturday: Sardines on toast, any cold meat with pickles, plain cake, fruit and cheese.

Chapter 18
Fish

The British shores, particularly the North Sea, have always been well supplied with the best kinds of fish. By the time of Edward II fish had, in England, become a delicacy, especially the sturgeon, which was permitted to appear on no table but that of the king. In the 14th century, a decree of King John informs us that the people ate both seals and porpoises during that period.

In Brillat Savarin's clever and amusing volumes *The Physiology of Taste,* he says that, towards the end of the 18th century, it was a most common thing for a well-arranged entertainment to commence with oysters, and that many guests were not content without swallowing 12 dozen.

Being anxious to know the weight of 12 dozen oysters, he ascertained that a dozen oysters, fluid included, weighed 4 ozs, the 12 dozen would then weight 3 lbs. An anecdote, perfectly well authenticated, is narrated of a French gentleman (M. Laperte), residing at Versailles, who was extravagantly fond of oysters, declaring that he never had enough. Savarin resolved to procure him the satisfaction and gave him an invitation to dinner which was duly accepted. The guest arrived and his host kept company with him in swallowing the delicious bivalves up to the tenth dozen, when, exhausted, he gave up and let M. Laperte go on alone. This gentleman managed to eat thirty two dozen within an hour and would doubtless have got through more but the person who opened them is described as not being very skilful. In the interim Savarin was idle, and at length, tired with his painful state of inaction, he said to Laperte, whilst the latter was in full career, "Mon cher, you will not eat as many oysters today as you meant; let us dine". They dined and the insatiable oyster eater acted at the repast as if he had fasted for a week.

71. Devilled Oysters

Popular today but more expensive, for 3 dozen it would have cost one penny in 1885. Oysters in season September to April.

3 dozen oysters, cayenne pepper, 6ozs best butter and salt to taste.
Open the oysters, but do not remove them from their shells. Under each oyster put cayenne pepper and salt according to your taste, and a small knob of butter on top. Put them under the grill for 3 minutes. Serve on a napkin, with brown bread and butter, with lemon wedge.

72. Tromps Oysters (Author's recipe)

I have always been a great admirer of a Master Chef of the 20th century, Silvino Trompetto M.B.E., who said, "The whole secret of life is not to know yourself, and for other people to know you even less!" (extract from *The Caterer & Hotelkeeper* November 17th 1977, when he was maitre chef de cuisine at The Savoy). He once wrote to me when I was a freelance chef, and told me "I do not agree with you when you say you are just an ordinary freelance chef. I am sure you are talented, and your clients must be more than satisfied". That made me work even harder in this wonderful trade.

2 dozen oysters on the half shell, 3ozs of chopped fennel, 3ozs of shallots, 2 cloves of garlic, 1 teaspoon of tarragon vinegar, ½lb of best butter ⅓ glass of old port, ⅓ glass of Tia Maria, salt and ground black pepper, chopped parsley and a whole lemon (all ingredients ground to a puree).

Saute the fennel, shallots in a little of the butter for 4 minutes, add all the above ingredients except the oysters, parsley and lemon. Reduce the sauce to ⅔rds, then pour a good heaped teaspoon over each oyster and bake in a moderate oven for 5 minutes, top with chopped parsley and serve with a wedge of lemon, brown bread and butter.

73. Barbecued Shrimp

This is a recipe that goes well at any party or fun gathering. It is a little expensive, but well worth it.

2lb of unshelled Mediterranean Crevettes (large), 1 clove of garlic minced, 2 tablespoons of crushed fennel seed, 6ozs of butter, 4ozs of cooking oil mixed, 1 tablespoon of paprika, 1 of basil, crushed bay leaves, chives, parsley, salt and ground black pepper.

Melt the butter with the oil and add all ingredients except the crevettes, mix thoroughly and when the sauce is just smoking drop in the crevettes, turning for 5 minutes until they are dark pink.

Arrange them on an oval dish dressed with lemon and parsley. Serve with a finger bowl. The sauce in a sauce boat with hot garlic bread arranged around it.

74. Sole Olivia

1 sole, 1 red pepper chopped fine, 3 chopped olives, 2 teaspoons of white wine, parsley sauce, lemon, salt and ground black pepper.

Skin and fillet the sole, season them well and put on the pepper, olives (chopped) and white wine, squeeze on the lemon juice, and bake in a moderate oven until it is flaky. Pour over the parsley sauce, garnish with parsley and lemon.

75. Old English Fish Chowder

¼lb of diced York ham, ¼lb of finely chopped onion, 1lb of diced potatoes, ½ pint of fish stock, 1lb of fillet haddock, ½ pint of cream, a teaspoonful of butter, a teaspoonful of chopped parsley, salt and pepper to taste.

Fry out the ham and onion until brown, add the potatoes, cook for a few minutes, then add the fish stock and cook until the potatoes are partly done. Now add the fish chopped fine. Cook for a further 20 minutes, season with the salt and pepper. Add the cream and let it cook through for a further 15 minutes. Top with a little butter and chopped parsley. Serve with toasted garlic bread.

Chapter 19
Luxury Eating

The Royal Pavilion, Brighton was redesigned (1815 – 23) by John (Beau) Nash in its Hindoo type style at a cost of £170,000. The hallmark as far as I am concerned is The Great Kitchen; a monument for English cookery.

The Prince of Wales, George or Prinny if you were a good friend of his, a stout and proud man, entertained thousands in the marvellous Banqueting Room with its Majestic chandelier which alone cost £6,000. He impressed everyone that ate there. He loved food and drink, he was proud of his kitchen and showed it off to everyone that visited the pavilion. Under the great pillars that looked like palm trees, was a range of equipment that would have pleased any chef of that period.

It is by referring to *The Frugal Housewife* of 1811 that we can discover today how they dressed a Turtle in the beginning of the nineteenth century or how they made Turtle Soup. It was served at all ceremonial dinners, diplomatic dinners, every Royal function, the aristocrats would put it on nearly every gala occasion. There are two types, Water and Land, the flesh of both can be eaten, Water Turtle is the one the English had imported from the West Indies, Australia, South America and Africa. These animals furnish the most delicious repast not only to the epicure but to all those who can obtain so luxurious a gratification. They are of various sizes, and that the reader may be informed how they dress them in 1800, we shall here confine ourselves to one of about 30 pounds in weight, observing that the same directions are to be proportionally attended to in dressing those of a more considerable size.

When you kill a turtle, which must be the night before you dress it, take off the head, and let it bleed two or three hours: then cut off the fins, and the callipee from the callipash, take care not to break the gall. Throw all the innards into cold water, the guts and tripe keep by themselves, and slit them open with a small knife; wash them very clean in scalding water, and scrape off all the inward skin; as you do them, throw them into cold water; wash them out of that, and put them in fresh water, and let them lie all night, scalding the fins and edges of the callipash and callipee; cut the meat off the shoulders, and hack the bones, and set them over the fire with the fins in about a quart of water, put a little mace, nutmeg, chyan and salt, let it stew about three hours, then strain it, and put the fins by for use. The next morning take some of the meat you cut off the shoulders, and chop it fine as for sausages, with about a pound of beef, season with mace, nutmeg, sweet marjoram, parsley, chyan, and salt to your taste, and three or four glasses of Madeira wine. Stuff it under the two pieces of fleshy parts of the meat, and if you have any left, lay it over to prevent the meat from burning; then cut the remainder of the meat and fins into pieces the size of an egg; season pretty high with chyan, salt and a little nutmeg, and put it into the callipash. Take care that it is sewed or secured up at the end, to keep in the gravy. Then boil up the gravy, and add more wine if required, and thicken it a little with butter and flour. Put some of it to the turtle, and set it in the oven with a well buttered paper over it to prevent it from burning, and when it is half baked, squeeze in the juice of two lemons, and stir it up. The callipash, or back, will take half an hour more baking than the callipee which will take two hours. The guts must be cut in pieces two inches long, the tripes in less, and put into a mug of clear water, set it in the oven with the callipash, and when it is enough drained from water, it is to be mixed with the other parts, and sent up very hot to the table. The cost of turtle was expensive at two shillings per pound, according to supply and demand.

"The destiny of nations," says Brillat Savarin, "depends on their diet". An opinion exactly coinciding with that of the ancient ballad-monger who asserted the infallibility of Britons so long as they were fed upon beef. Without exactly assenting either to the gastronomic Frenchman or the British bard, we are of opinion that the civilization of a people or of an age may be ascertained by the style of its cuisine. Man has been defined as a cooking animal; and his pre-eminence in the art is asuredly a sign of his advancement.

Gastronomic taste changes with the progress of the people. In bluff King Henry VIII's days a porpoise was esteemed a delicacy, and sent with great care to the royal table. The seasoning of dishes was strong and pungent; saffron being a predominating ingredient in them.

Shakespeare gives us some inkling of Elizabethan cookery in the Winter Tale, where the clown, sent shopping by the sweet Perdita for the sheep-shearing feast, says:—

"Three pound of sugar; five pound of currants; rice? — what will this sister of mine do with rice? But my father hath made her mistress of the feast, and she lays it on! ... I must have saffron to colour the warden-pies (pear pies) mace, dates, nutmegs seven — a race or two of ginger (but may I beg); four pounds of prunes, and as many raisins of the sun.''

Lord Bacon enumerates as the fruits of an Elizabethan dessert — pears, apricots, barberries, filberts, musk melons, grapes, apples peaches, melocobones, nectarine, cornelians, wardens (of which Perditas pies were made), quinces and medlars. Some of these horticultural rarities are extinct now, like the sweet old flowers of that age, they have passed away before the more cultivated and improved fruits of the advancing centuries.

The fee-favour of the city of Norwich was twenty-four herring-pies, each containing five herrings. They were carried to Court by the Lord of the Manor of Carleton. These pies were seasoned with a half a pound of ginger, half a pound of pepper, a quarter of cinnamon, one ounce of cloves, one ounce of long pepper, half an ounce of grains of paradise, and half a pound of gantegals — whatever they may have been. Grains of Paradise (employed in modern times, we have been told, by publicans for doctoring their beer, and increasing the thirst of their customers — modern times being 1868) were much used in those days of strong palates, being very pungent and pepper.

Tea and coffee must have been great softeners of the national mood we fancy, in spite of George III, who of course had such a gentle diet. But what dinners were those under which the boards of the great groaned in his days!

The singular succession of dishes strikes us. 'Oysters, — a 'Sir Loyn of Beef, — a shoulder of veal; — then fish dressed with claret; tongue, pigeons, cowcumbers, fritters, almond pudding, and soup!''

After the soup is removed, venison pasty, *black pudding,* hare, and goose! Ale and claret formed the liquid part of this substantial meal.

Looking back to *Cooks Dictionary and Accomplished House-wifes Companion* of that period, we are amazed at the coarseness of our more recent forefathers' cookery. A gammon of bacon was to be boiled with hay tied up in a cloth in the water in which it was cooked; the hay being supposed to give it a good flavour.

Bacon Tart was another dish revolting to modern taste, being made of melted bacon fat, artichoke bottoms, macaroons and eggs, seasoned with salt, pepper, beaten cinnamon and sugar, and iced with sugar and orange-flower water.

A neck of lamb was fried with ale, which appears to have been greatly used in the kitchens at that time, as well as rosemary, alkanet root, etc.

Indeed simplicity, always the perfection of an art, was evidently unknown to the Duke of Bolton's Chef-de-Cuisine, who edited the said *Cooks Dictionary*.

Chapter 20
Game

76. Rabbits Surprised (1811)
Take *two young rabbits,* skewer them and put the same kind of *pudding* into them as for roasted rabbits. When they are roasted take off the meat clean from the bones; but leave the bones whole. Chop the meat very fine, with *a little shred parsley, some lemon peel, an ounce of beef marrow, a spoonful of cream and a little salt.* Beat up *the yolks of two eggs boiled hard, and a small piece of butter,* in a marble mortar; then mix all together and put it into a stew pan. Having stewed it five minutes lay it on the rabbits where you took the meat off, and put it close down with your hand, to make them appear like whole rabbits. Then with a salamander brown them all over. Pour a *good brown gravy,* made as thick as cream, into the dish, and stick a *bunch of myrtle* in their mouths. Send them up to the table with their livers boiled and frothed.

77. Baked Rabbit Pudding (Alexis Soyer 1830)
First boil *a rabbit* until tender, then remove the bones and cut the meat into small pieces. Make *a piece of suet crust with ¼lb flour, 5ozs chopped suet, salt and pepper and enough water* to make a rather stiff paste. Line a greased pudding basin with the pastry (put to one side).

Put the rabbit into a saucepan with *1oz butter* and lightly fry *with chopped chives, a pinch of cayenne pepper, salt and pepper, a glass of red wine and a little stock* from the boiled rabbit. Add *a spoonful of flour* to thicken. Bring to the boil for 10 minutes, let it simmer for 5 minutes, then put it into the basin and cover with a suet crust. Bake in a moderate oven for an hour (gas 5).

78. Larks *Young Woman's Companion or Frugal Housewife* 1811
Take *a dozen of larks,* put them on a skewer, and tie both ends of the skewer to the spit. Dredge and baste them, and in about ten or twelve minutes they will be done. Make your sauce thus: take the crumb of *a half penny loaf,* shred it very fine, and put it into a saucepan, with *a piece of butter* about the size of a walnut. Shake it over a gentle fire till it is of a light brown, then lay it between your birds on your plate or dish, and pour a little melted butter over them.

79. Woodcocks or Snipes *Frugal Housewife* 1811

These birds are so peculiar from all others, that they must never be drawn. When you have spitted them, take *the round of a three-penny loaf,* and toast it nice and brown; then lay it in a dish under the birds, and when you put them in the fire, baste them with a *little butter,* and let the trail or gut drop on the toast. When they are done, put the toast in the dish, and lay the birds on it. Pour about a quarter of a pint of *gravy* into the dish, and set it over a lamp or chafing dish for three to four minutes, and then take it hot to the table. A woodcock will take about twenty minutes roasting, and a snipe fifteen.

I enjoy venison. A good friend of mine, Martin Scott, who is an excellent shot, took me to Scotland with him some time ago, on a stag shoot. I only lasted half a day, the mountains we had to climb to bring back the venison tired me out after just a few miles. Martin must have climbed over 65 miles that week we were in Glen Lyon, on the Roro Estate. He brought home two stags and did the traditional toast of success with a bottle of the finest scotch whisky. There are three kinds of venison in Great Britain, the red deer, the fallow deer, and the roebuck, peculiar to Scotland as the red deer now is to Ireland.

The flesh of the fallow deer is the best. Venison should be dark, finely grained and firm, with a good coating of fat. I usually hang a beast from 2 – 3 weeks, longer for a red deer. It will take 15 to 20 minutes per pound to roast and cooked at 190C or gas mark 5, basteing it frequently. Sprinkled with rosemary and fennel seed a saddle of young venison would take about 80 minutes. When we got back from Scotland my butcher sectioned the venison up and with the ribs we did barbecued venison ribs which Martin had never had before. There were over 7lb so I cut them up into lengths of six inches and placed them in a very large baking tray.

80. Barbecued Venison Ribs (Author's recipe)

Then I made a sauce as follows: *1 bottle of red wine, 1 pint of cider, 2 teaspoons of finely minced root ginger, 1 whole garlic (crushed), ¼ pint of soy sauce, 3 tablespoons of finely crushed fennel seed, 1lb of clear honey, and a few drops of red colouring.* Mix all the above ingredients together and pour over the ribs. Cook the ribs in a moderate oven for 2 hours. Place the ribs with the sauce in a cool room for 48 hours. Now remove the ribs and place into another baking tray. Put the sauce through a fine sieve and pour into a large saucepan, bring to the boil and reduce by ¼. Add a little *cornflour with milk and sherry* to slightly thicken the sauce. Pour over the ribs and return to the oven for 45 minutes 190C or gas mark 5. Now you can have a Venison Rib party.

One of the ancient customs of the Scots was that of boiling the flesh of the animals they killed "in the skin of the beast, filling the same full of water". So far back as the 14th century they did not use pots or pans but stretched the beasts on four stakes and filled their bellies with water. What closer parallel could be found to this custom of cooking an animal in its own skin than the favourite modern 'haggis' of our northern neighbours, which is a hash of the liver, heart and lungs of a sheep minced in its own maw.

Haggis along with porridge or cock-a-leekie soup is one of the national dishes of Scotland, at large banquets it is escorted by pipers.

81. Haggis

1 sheeps paunch and pluck, (1 heart, liver and lungs), 1 pinch of nutmeg, cayenne, ground black pepper and salt, 1lb oatmeal, 1lb suet, 2lbs chopped onions.

Take the sheep's paunch and pluck clean it thoroughly in salted water, take the heart, liver and lungs of the sheep. Boil them for 30 minutes in salt water. Take out the offal and mince it very finely, except for part of the liver which must be allowed to get cold so that it can be chopped.

Mix all together and add the oatmeal, suet, finely chopped onions and seasoning. Press the mixture lightly into the paunch and sew up the opening, allowing for the oatmeal to swell. Place into a large pan of boiling water for 3 hours.

Chapter 21
Great Chefs

Antonin Careme (1784-1833) who was with the Prince Regent for two years, and wrote a number of cookery books, was famous for his artistic manner and elaborate dishes (e.g. Apple Charlotte). His *L'art de la Cuisine francaise au-dix-neuvième siècle* in three volumes was the standard work on French cuisine. He started work at the age of fifteen as a kitchen help and had the exceptional qualities needed to be a Master of his trade. While working for the Prince Regent, later King George IV, every morning Careme would explain the properties to his Royal Master of each individual dish. The Prince exclaimed to him one day, "You will kill me with a surfeit of food, I have a fancy for everything you put before me. The temptation is far too great!" "Your Highness," came his reply (he relates this conversation in the preamble to his *Cuisinier Parisien),* "my great concern is to stimulate your appetite by the variety of my dishes. It is no concern of mine to curb it."

Laurent Tailhade said he worked himself to death, or burnt himself out by the flame of his genius and the fuel of his ovens. He hated the British weather, the one reason why the £2,000 to stay with the Prince Regent could not tempt him. He died on January 12th 1833.

The French have always possesed an instinctive knowledge of the chemistry of cooking, hence their unrivalled excellence in the art. Here is an extract on the subject, translated from Careme's *L'Art de la Cuisine Francaise:*—

> The good housewife, puts her meat into an earthen stock-pot and pours cold water on it, in the proportion of two quarts to three pounds of the beef. She sets it at the side of the fire . . . and unconsciously performs an act of chemical skill. The pot grows gradually hot, and as the water heats it dilates the muscular fibres of the flesh by dissolving the gelatinous matter which covers them; and allows the albumen to detach itself easily, and rise to the surface of the water in light foam or scum while the osmazone, which is the savoury juice of the meat, dissolving little by little adds flavour to the broth. By this simple proceeding of slow cooking, the housewife obtains a savoury and nourishing broth, and a bouille (boiled meat) tender and with a good flavour. These are the results of the chemical action of fire; but, by placing the pot-au-feu on too hot a fire, it boils too soon; the albumen coagulates and hardens; the water not having had the time necessary to penetrate the meat,

hinders the osmazone from disengaging itself, and the sad result is that you have only a hard piece of boiled meat and a broth without flavour or goodness.

A little fresh water poured into the pot at intervals helps the scum to rise more abundantly.

Rosa Lewis

My favourite cook still is Rosa Lewis (the original Duchess of Duke Street) who said 'I learnt to think that it was not a stupid thing to cook, I cooked because I loved to cook, the money didn't matter'. Born in 1867 Rosa Ovenden, Rosa started service as a general servant in 1879 for a middle class Victorian family, Mr and Mrs Ralph Musgrave of No. 3 Myrtle Villas, London for a shilling a week. She worked hard for that shilling starting at 6.00 am.

She would clean the grates, lay a new fire and light it, tidy all the rooms downstairs, wash lino and tiled hall, sweep the stairs and carpets, cook breakfast and lay the table, wash the front steps, polish the letter box, door knob and key plate, wait for the Musgraves to come in for breakfast at 7.00 am.

She would then take instruction from Mrs Musgrave for the shopping list. Then wash the breakfast dishes, clean and polish the furniture, clean windows, forks and spoons, empty the chamberpots, wash herself, change her apron and prepare for luncheon and lay the table.

After the family had had lunch she would wash all the dishes, have a snack herself and change from her grey uniform to her black afternoon uniform.

Prepare afternoon tea and homemade biscuits, serve and clear them away. Wash up and prepare dinner for 7.00 sharp. After dinner had finished which could take them 2 hours she would clear the table, wash up, tidy the kitchen for the morning. Put out a nightcap for the Musgrave family and she would then go to bed herself.

Her other duties of course included the Monday wash, with the soap and scrubbing board, which she hated, because she had all the other problem jobs to do as well. She stayed with the Musgraves for a four year period.

Rosa's next job was at the aristocratic household of the exiled heir to the French throne, the Comte de Paris, for a weekly wage of twelve shillings. She was determined to climb the ladder of progress. She would work her little fingers to the bone through the domestic service to become her dream ambition, a cook and one that would be remembered, independent and famous. Her rise was fast.

The Comte de Paris, born in 1838, had gone into exile with his father in 1848 to England. From the age of 10 to 21 he lived at Sheen House which his father bought near Mortlake. In 1888 the Comte became head of the house of Bourbon and was accepted by the Royalist party as France's rightful King. The corpse of King Louis Philippe had been returned to France by his family and this, with the Comte's acceptance by the Royalists, served to infuriate the republicans. All of this happened while Rosa was working at Sheen House. Rosa learned a lot from Sheen House. Being the only English member of the staff she learned the French language, and the culinary arts of French cuisine.

Edward, the Prince of Wales, was a regular visitor to Sheen House, and because the pianist was absent the Comte asked Rosa to sing 'God bless the Prince of Wales.' Rosa did this even though everyone was drunk. The Prince mistook Rosa for the cook and gave her a sovereign. It was to be 5 years before she left Sheen House. During the five years Rosa was lent out to the Duc d'Aumale, the son of Louis Philippe the Comte's uncle, who had a large palace at Chatilly. From there she experienced more cookery knowledge and lived a life of pure fantasy with its Greek temples, racecourse, lakes and waterfalls and a moat all around the chateau. Rosa returned to England to be loaned out again to another French exile, the Comte's son, the Duke of Orleans, at Sandhurst as temporary cook. Rosa showed her ability to the fullest extent and gained respect from the French staff at Sandhurst, which must have been very hard, considering most of the palaces had chefs and Rosa had to prove her worth. Although cooks were on the top rung of the ladder and the kitchen was their castle their food had to make the impression. In Rosa's case she got a glowing reference in 1887 when she left the Comte's employ. She went like all good cooks and chefs do to an agency where she found Lady Randolph Churchill needed a relief cook for her overworked chef on his days off.

She was brimming with confidence, and determined to get the job. Lady Churchill was one of the top society hostesses of the century. Everyone wanted to be at 50 Grosvenor Square, the mecca of social activity. Rosa had met the Prince of Wales quite a few times, and he had praised her cooking ability. The Prince, said Rosa, only liked plain simple cooking, nothing fancy and nothing added, his favourite being truffles. She was gaining more and more experience, accounts, stock control, general management of the kitchen. She left the Churchills and worked in a variety of establishments gaining more and more experience.

Rosa Lewis *(B.B.C. Hulton Picture Library)*

She worked for numerous people from Lord Savile, (Augustus Lumley), who was Master of Ceremonies to Queen Victoria's household, Margot Asquith, Lord Ribblesdale and many more.

Rosa had a marriage of convenience at Trinity Church in 1893 to Excelsior Lewis who was a butler to the Honourable Sir Andrew Clarke. Rosa started freelance catering which Excelsior did not like and was very jealous about. For five years the business grew and the name Rosa Lewis spread like wild fire. During the later periods Rosa became an admirer of the King of Chefs Escoffier and was to become a firm friend of his. This was only the beginning of the Rosa Lewis success story which went on to when she bought the since famous Cavendish Hotel in Jermyn Street for the sum of £5,000.

Auguste Escoffier was born in a charming town in the Alpes Maritimes, Villeneuve-Loubet in 1847. He began his career at the age of twelve, and became a very great chef. In 1890, in association with Ritz and Echenard, two masters of the hotel business, he opened the Savoy Hotel in London, and remained in this illustrious establishment until 1898, when, for personal reasons, he gave up the direction of the Savoy kitchens to take charge of those of the Carleton Hotel, then one of the most famous in Europe. As a reward for all he had done to enhance the prestige of French cooking through-out the world, Escoffier was made a Chevalier of the Legion of Honour and Officer of the Legion.

Escoffier's culinary career was brilliant. He was regarded as the emperor of the world's kitchens, a title conferred upon him by the Emperor William II, who spent some time on the steamer Imperator of the Hamburg-American Line, which Escoffier had joined to take charge of the imperial kitchens.

In the course of conversation with Escoffier, the Emperor, congratulating him, said; 'I am the Emperor of Germany, but you are the Emperor of chefs'.

Escoffier retired in 1921. He was then 74 years of age and had practised his art for sixty two years. In all the history of cookery, there is no other example of such a long professional career. He died in February 1935, nearly 89 years old.

The culinary writings of Escoffier are works of authority.

The best-known are le Guide Culinaire, written in collaboration with Phileas Gilbert and Emile Fetu; le Livre des menus; les Fleurs en cire; Ma cuisine; le Ritz; le Carnet d'Epicure.

It was Escoffier who, in 1893, honoured the Australian singer, Nellie Melba, by creating the peach dish that bears her name. He

Auguste Escoffier *(B.B.C. Hulton Picture Library)*

also invented the dodine au Chambertin and the chaud-froid Jeanette, the latter named after a ship that was trapped in the Polar ice. Many delicate culinary creations are associated with his name. *Ma Cuisine* has at long last become available in English translated from French by Vyvyan Holland.

Alexis Soyer (1809-1858)

Alexis Soyer was born in Neaux-en-Brie, France. Son of a shop-keeper, he trained as a commis for four years at Chez Grignon in Paris. He then went to work at the La Maison Doix and after only a year's service was made Head Chef. When the revolution of 1848 started in France, Alexis fled to England to become one of the famous chefs of his time being appointed chef at the Reform Club, the kitchen of which he designed himself. He was the first chef in England to do mass catering. His ideas went before Queen Victoria who was very impressed with the way he sorted out the appalling Army catering facilities. He trained the Army cooks on hygiene and showed them how to make a banquet out of army rations and brought dignity back to the cookhouse during the Crimean War in 1855. Out of his own pocket he paid all expenses incurred. Many cookery books he had published all sold extremely well; *Gastronomic Regenerator, The Modern Housewife, The Poor Man's Regenerator, A Shilling Cookery;* his Crimean books *Soyer's Culinary Campaign* and *Instructions to Military Hospital Cooks* all sold in their thousands.

With Crosse & Blackwell he made bottled sauces, Soyer's Lady & Gentleman's sauce — followed by Soyer's Relish at two shillings & sixpence a bottle and a bottled fruit juice called Soyer's Nectar.

His Magic Stove, which was the first stove for cooking in the dining room, was praised by all the gourmets, chefs and writers. He demonstrated its use on the top of the Great Pyramid in Egypt. It is the prototype of the lamp used for table cookery in the restaurants of today.

At the age of 49, with Crimean fever, he died at his house in St. John's Wood, London and was buried at Kensal Green cemetery in August 1858.

On pages 55 and 143 are recipes of Soyer's that he did in the kitchens of Florence Nightingale's hospital at Scutari when he was at the peak of his career.

Alexis Benoit Soyer *(B.B.C. Hulton Picture Library)*

Soyer's Patent Culinary Utensils.

It would be unjust to the memory of a great cook if we omitted from our list the culinary utensils invented by the late M. Soyer, to whom our gratitude as a nation is due. They consist of the Baking Stewing Pan, the Improved Baking Dish, the Vegetable Drainer, and the Portfolio Meat Screen.

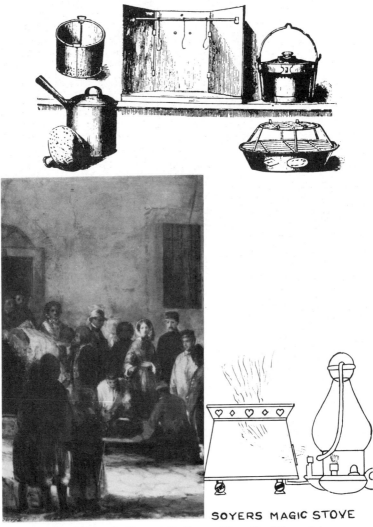

(top) Soyer's Patent Culinary Utensils *(Warne's)*;
(bottom left) Soyer (under window) with Florence Nightingale *(National Potrait Gallery)*; *(bottom right)* Soyer's Magic Stove *(a drawing by the author's brother)*

76

A more modern Flambé Lamp

Chapter 22
Sauces

Dishes to a great extent depend upon the qualities of sauces for success. It is probably correct to rank sauce-making amongst the very highest branches of the art, and to regard it as worthy of the most careful study, and skill and discrimination on the part of the cook. Gravy and sauces are sometimes classed as one, but in practice it is perhaps best to limit the term gravy to meat juice in whatever way obtained and however variously treated, provided it is served thin or slightly thickened.

There are a vast variety of sauces, and the greatest care should be employed in selecting the appropriate one for each dish. The marked success of sauces in many cases is due to the prolonged cooking which they undergo. The mistake is too often made of hurrying the preparation, not giving time for the flour to cook thoroughly, the flavours to become properly blended and the sauce to assume its perfect condition of velvety smoothness.

Sometimes a direction is given to allow a sauce to boil, but this should only apply when eggs are not used. The great chefs and cooks of the 19th century would have considered the basic roux an essential factor of cookery, for without it you have nothing.

Basic Roux

A roux is a combination of melted fat and flour, the flour being added to the melted fat and cooked with or without a colouring. Mixing the flour to the fat allows the flour to cook evenly, and when the stock is added, makes a smooth velvety sauce. The roux can be basically prepared in three different ways.

82. 1. White Roux

Heat *a 1lb of butter* in a medium saucepan, stir in a *1lb of plain flour* and mix. Cook it very slowly under a low heat until it becomes a light sandy colour. This is now ready for a basic white sauce.

83. 2. Blond Roux

Prepare and cook in the same manner as for the white roux, with the faintest tint of colouring for a velouté and tomato sauce.

84. 3. Brown Roux
Prepared and cooked in the same manner as for white roux. The fat used should be good quality dripping from the roast meat, and increase the flour by 20%. Cook it to a light brown chocolate colour. This is used for a basic brown sauce and brown soups such as liver and kidney.

85. Variations of White Sauce
Adding the ingredients to the white roux gives you the following different sauces.

Anchovy sauce	Using fish stock add 2 teaspoons of anchovy essence and a teaspoonful of lemon juice.
Caper sauce	Use fish stock or beef stock for meat, 2 tablespoons of capers, and 2 vinegar from the capers.
Cheese sauce	Using all milk, add 3 heaped tablespoons of dry, grated cheese, salt, pepper and a little mustard.
Herb sauce	2 heaped tablespoons of mixed herbs of your choice depending on meat or fish, use less for fish.
Mushroom sauce	2ozs chopped mushrooms cooked in the butter, then add the flour and cook out, using milk and stock.
Onion sauce	2 onions finely chopped, salt and black pepper (same method as mushroom).
Parsley sauce	1 tablespoon of chopped parsley.
Shrimp sauce	3ozs of shrimps chopped fine, same as mushroom adding 1 teaspoon of lemon juice and ½ of anchovy essence.

86. Béchamel sauce
1 small carrot, 1 small onion, 1 stick of celery, 2 bay leaves, 4 peppercorns, 3 tablespoons of cream, salt and pepper to season.
Slice the vegetables, cover them and the spices with a pint of milk or as much as it needs to cover. Bring them slowly to the boil, remove from the heat and let them infuse in the liquid for ¾ *hour. Strain the milk and use it to make the white sauce. Stir the cream into the boiling sauce.*

Walnut Ketchup

A traditional English sauce of great character based on fine flavour of Black walnuts, this recipe is from Warnes Model Cookery 1868, possibly taken from George Watkins famous recipe of 1830. The cost of making this recipe would be about £6.00. You can purchase this product today for around fifty pence, in 1830 it would have cost 2d.

87. Walnut Ketchup (Warnes *Model Cookery* 1868)
100 black walnuts, 6ozs shallots, 1 head of garlic, ½lb of salt, 2 qts of vinegar, 2ozs anchovies, 2ozs pepper, ¼oz of mace, ½oz of cloves.

Beat in a large mortar a hundred black walnuts until they are thoroughly broken, then put them into a jar with 6ozs shallots cut into pieces, a head of garlic, 2 quarts of vinegar, and the ½lb of salt; let them stand for 2 weeks, stirring them twice a day. Strain off the liquor, put it into a stew pan with the anchovies, whole peppers, ½oz of cloves and a ¼ of mace; boil it skimming it well. Strain it off, and when cold pour it clear from any sediments into small bottles, cork it down tight and store it in a dry place. The sediment can be used for flavouring sauces.

88. Anchovy Sauce

This recipe from 1811 has many uses with poached or grilled fish, anchovy butter, fish pie and my favourite, adding a tablespoon in with the mixture of fish cakes.

4 anchovies, ¼lb of best butter, 1 teacup of water, a spoonful of vinegar and a little flour.

Chop up the anchovies, melt the butter and water in a saucepan, bring to the boil and add the vinegar and a little flour to thicken, stirring all the time so it does not go lumpy. I suggest you do this recipe as a roux then add the anchovies.

89. Prince Regents Sauce Marie-Antoine Careme
One ounce of Cayenne, one quart of vinegar, 6 cloves, one gill of mushroom ketchup, one gill of soy, a small quantity of anchovy.

Mix it well, shake it daily for 10 days, strain and bottle it.

90. Royal Sauce for Fish *The Domestic Cookery* 1806
Four yolks of eggs, half a pound of fresh butter, one dessertspoonful of elder vinegar, two teaspoonfuls of tarragon vinegar, a spoonful of chilli vinegar, a teaspoonful of soy, a very little mace.

Beat up four yolks of eggs with half pound of butter, mix with it the above ingredients, add a few tiny pieces of butter not mixed. Then stand your stewpan inside another and larger one, resting it on pieces of wood placed across the bottom of the large stewpan, so that the water will surround the lesser one. Put the two saucepans on the fire, turning the one that contains the sauce till it becomes of smooth thickness. If too thick, add a little more elder vinegar. It is best to serve this sauce the instant it is made.

91. Royal Sauce
If you omit the soy and mace you have what is commonly known as Hollandaise with the added extras of *6 tablespoons of white wine, cayenne pepper, chopped chervil, chopped tarragon, 2 teaspoons chopped shallot, and salt, pepper (pinch).*

Put the wine, vinegar, herbs, shallots, seasoning and 10oz butter into a saucepan and boil until reduced by ⅔rds. Remove from the heat and leave it to cool for a few minutes. Add 3 egg yolks and return to a very low heat. Gradually add 8ozs of softened butter (melted) and stir with a whisk (not forgetting to stand your pan inside another with boiling water). The binding of the sauce is produced by the slow cooking of the egg yolks, so it is important to make Royal sauce over a very low heat. When the butter has blended, strain the sauce through a muslin; season with cayenne and add the chervil and tarragon.

92. Mushroom Catchup
Take a quantity of the *full grown flaps of mushrooms,* crush them well with your hands, and then stew *a quantity of salt* all over them. Let them stand all night and the next day put them into stew-pans. Set them in a quick oven for twelve hours and then strain them through a hair sieve. To every gallon of liquor put *of cloves, Jamaica, black pepper and ginger, one ounce each,* and a *half a pound of common salt.* Set it on a slow fire and let it boil till half the liquor is wasted away. Then put it into a clean pot and when it is quite cold bottle it for use.

George Watkins Meeting House Emblem, which was in 1830 and still is today the sign for quality pickles and sauces, with a variety of labels used over the years.

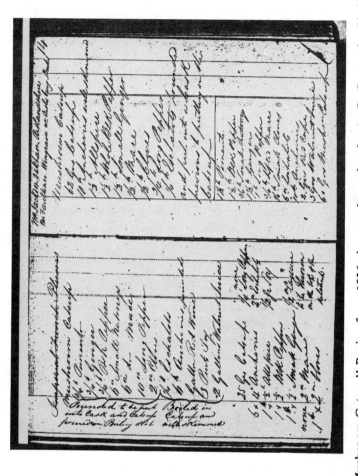

The orginal "Mushroom Catsup" Recipe from 1836 given to the author by A. G. Costa, the Chairman of Keddie Limited. They took over the George Watkins business in 1923.

93. Mushroom Ketchup

Mushrooms from the market is advisable. Mushrooms for this purpose must be dry. Break them up into small pieces, place them in an ovenware dish, and sprinkle with salt, *allowing ¼ lb of salt* to each 4lb of chopped mushrooms (button). Let them stand for at least 3 days, frequently stirring and mashing them to cause the juice to rise. Now strain and also get all the juice possible by squeezing them. To each quart of juice add *2ozs of salt, a few cloves, a pinch of cayenne and a little mace.* Boil slowly for 1½ hours, then strain. Bottle, cork well, and wax the corks over with a candle.

Geo Watkins Mushroom Ketchup which you can still buy today for about 50p a bottle was being used from 1830, which was the secret success of many Victorian cooks with steak and kidney pies and their roast meats. According to *The Caterer* from 1878, mushrooms varied in price from a penny to sixpence per pound.

94. Mayonnaise Sauce Escoffier (1860)

Most of the compound cold sauces start with mayonnaise which, for that reason, is considered a 'mother-sauce' in the same way as espagnole and velouté sauces. The making of mayonnaise is very simple but one must pay attention to certain rules as shown in the following method:

3-4 yolks, (with thread removed) ¼ oz fine salt, pinch of white pepper, 1 teaspoon of tarragon vinegar, 2 teaspoons Dijon mustard (optional), 1 pint oil, 2 hot water (tablespoons).

Put the egg yolks into a basin, add the salt, pepper, a little of the vinegar and mustard. Stir the eggs with a whisk, add the oil very slowly to begin with going a little faster as it begins to bind.

Add a few drops of vinegar from time to time. Finally add the boiling water, the object of which is to ensure cohesion and to prevent it from curdling if it has to be kept.

The causes of curdling are as follows:
1. Too rapid addition of oil at the beginning.
2. Employing oil which is too cold (chefs and cooks today use it warm).
3. Too much oil for the number of eggs used.

Chapter 23
Inns and Hotels

Early Inns

Instead of numbers to mark the different shops and dwelling houses, signs swung and creaked above each door. These are now confined chiefly to inns; but the Golden Key, the Blue Boar, the Spread Eagle, and similar signs shone then with bright variety along every street.

There were numerous hackney-coaches, but the sedan-chair was the favourite mode of conveyance in the city. Then the Inn keeper had to have the patience of a saint, he had to be a handyman and a man of knowledge, if he was hit over the head with a tankard, I am sure he would not have sworn but said "thank you . . ."

If a visitor was one of class he would have signed his name in the Visitors' Book which then was a valuable testimony to the goodwill of the Inn.

Most people put nice things in such a book, but the poet Wordsworth was an exception for when asked at the *Lion Hotel* Dolgelly, to put some remarks in the book there, he wrote the following:—

> "If you ever should visit Dolgelly,
> Don't stay at the Lion Hotel,
> For there's nothing to put in your belly,
> And no one to answer the bell".

As the *Lion Hotel* is still a famous house, let me say at once that the words were written many years ago. The innkeeper would provide a meal of meat and vegetables followed by cheese with a jug of beer that would cost two pennies, hay and corn fourpence. The servant would see to the horses and would usually sleep with them, after being fed on bread, mutton with cheese and water to follow.

Milk porridge would be served to the gentleman followed by ham with scrambled eggs. This looks like a rosy picture but some of the Inns were really bad. The wine was undrinkable, the smell was of fowls or stinking partridges and cow dung was an everyday hazard.

The word sanitation was not known, they would scratch and spit while having a breakfast of cold mutton and beer, while on the other side of the Inn men would be watching a cockfight.

When the railways started in 1830 the Inn was at its peak of prosperity. But as the railways grew and grew, the Inn started to decline. Terminal and posting inns were disappearing, as their position, based as it was on the halting and incoming traffic, rarely coincided with the new railway routes and terminals. Hotels followed to a great extent the pattern of location laid down by the railway stations. The giants were the terminal railway hotels, *The Midland Grand* adjoining St. Pancras station with 470 rooms, *The Euston Hotel,* 250 rooms, *Great Eastern* at Liverpool St., 250 rooms, *Charing Cross,* 450 rooms, and the famous Savoy, Victoria Carleton and Claridges which were for the rich and famous.

Clubs were also becoming the meeting places of the upper classes to eat and drink. They were great places where women could not enter. The club became an Established British Institution and still is so today. They do let women in most of the clubs today, but it was not until late into the nineteenth century that the clubs began to open their doors to women.

Chapter 24
Potatoes

The Value of the Potato

In 1563 Sir John Hawkins is said to have introduced the potato into England, but its cultivation was neglected and it was reintroduced in 1586 by Sir Francis Drake. Sir Walter Raleigh grew potatoes in Ireland.

In 1619 potatoes were among the foods to be served at the Royal table in England. It did not, however, become an article of import until 1662. The potato is an energy Food, 100 calories per 100g. (4ozs), rich in carbohydrates and in vitamins B & C. After its popularisation, thanks to Parmentier, the potato became one of the staple foods at the beginning of the nineteenth century.

I think it is one of the most under-rated items in the vegetable family; the most important of all vegetables. There are many varieties of potatoes, and hundreds of ways to prepare them. Potatoes with a waxy, rather yellowish pulp are best for frying and the whiter and softer ones for boiling or baking.

The methods of the early nineteenth century are still used today along with the recipes.

95. Potatoes *The Frugal Housewife* 1811

These must be boiled in so small a quantity of water as will be just sufficient to keep the saucepan from burning. Keep them close covered, and as soon as the skins begin to crack, they are enough. Having drained out all the water, let them remain in the saucepan covered for 2 or 3 minutes; then peel them, lay them in a plate, and pour some *melted butter* over them. Or, when you have peeled them, you may do thus: lay them on a gridiron till they are of fine brown, and send them to table.

96. Potato Ribbons 1835

4 large potatoes washed remove any eyes, lay them in warm water for 15 minutes. Then peel them like you would an apple; but do not cut the curls too thin, or they are likely to break. Fry them very slowly in butter until a light brown, and drain them from the grease. Pile the ribbons up on a hot dish, sprinkle with fresh parsley and serve.

97. Potato Puffs 1868

3ozs of flour, 3ozs brown sugar; 3 large well boiled potatoes, ½ oz butter, 2 eggs, a little grated nutmeg.

Boil and mash the potatoes, mix all the ingredients together well. Make them into small cakes, fry till a golden brown and serve with a white sauce.

98. Potatoes Au Gratin Dauphinoise Auguste Escoffier 1890

2lb potatoes, freshly ground pepper, a pinch of nutmeg, salt, 1 egg, 1 pint of boiled milk, grated Gruyère cheese, butter and garlic.

Peel and slice the potatoes thinly. Put into a bowl with salt, pepper, beaten egg, nutmeg, milk and 3ozs grated cheese, Mix all well together. Rub a casserole round with garlic, butter well and put in the potato mixture. Sprinkle with grated cheese until covered. Cook in a moderate oven Gas 4, 350F.

99. Susan's Potatoes

2lb potatoes, (cooked and mashed), 1 onion chopped fine and fried, 1 egg, ¼ pint of cream, 1oz of butter, pinch of nutmeg, 3ozs grated cheese, 1oz parsley salt and pepper to taste. 1 complete mixture of homemade stuffing dried.

Mix all the ingredients together, and make them into small balls, except the stuffing, with a bowl of egg wash (1 egg mixed with 6 tablespoons of milk), dip the ball into the egg then the stuffing, do this twice to make sure the stuffing is thick. Deep fry until golden brown, serve with any main course.

Chapter 25
Kitchen Equipment

Roasting: The cook would prepare the fire about 2 hours before she would put the roast on the fire. The success of roasting depended on the heat and goodness of the fire. It was a regular occurrence to send nearly raw meat or dried up meat to the table because the fire was not attended to properly.

Roasting is cooking by direct rays from a heat source. It was originally done on what was called a 'Jack'. A particularly efficient type of roasting jack was one involving a weight fastened to a chain. The weight was wound up to a good height on a pulley and then allowed to fall slowly floorwards. As it dropped a spit was turned by a further system of pulleys. The spit impaled the meat to be roasted and as it revolved in front of the blazing logs the joint, or possibly the whole beast, was roasted evenly and gradually. Normally a pan was placed below the spit to catch the falling fat, this was then poured back over the joint by a boy called the 'baster scullion'.

When it was done the baster scullion would make a gravy by adding herbs and salt to what was left in the pan.

The length of time required for baking or roasting depends on the kind of meat and the thickness of the joint. Generally speaking, beef requires 15 minutes to the pound, mutton, lamb and veal 20 minutes, but pork because of the closeness of the fibres must be baked for 25 minutes to the pound.

When roasting it is important to conserve the juices and goodness. This is done by putting the meat into a very hot oven of about 480F at first to seal and harden the outside. Cooking is then continued at a more moderate heat.

Cradle spits were much used in the large kitchens; for the small kitchen they used a bottle-jack, to the more modern a Spring Jack and roaster (1860s).

The finest invention of this period was the cooking range, which was either a hotplate heated by fire or the gas cooker which Alexis Soyer had introduced to the Reform Club in the 1830s. Pall Mall was alight by gas as early as 1807.

From *The Caterer and Refreshment Contractors Gazette April 6th, 1878*

Gas Cookery

The use of gas for cooking purposes formed the subject of repeated experiments after its utility as an illuminating agent had become demonstrated beyond all question, but it was not until 1831 that theory became reduced to practice in the shape of certain improvements in culinary apparatus for which the inventor, Mr Robert Hicks, obtained patent rights. These improvements consisted in placing in a recess, close to the chimney of the ordinary range, a table fitted with stands and burners for gas jets. The burners were arranged in the form of rings, and over them a kind of hood, for carrying off the vapour of the gas by means of the chimney with which it was connected.

Through the centre of the ring burner rose an upright spit, in such a manner that a joint of meat placed on it became exposed to the action of the gas-jets. For basting a small colander was fitted to the top of each hood, and joined to it was a funnel, by means of which gravy can be poured into the colander and thence onto the meat. This method was found efficient, so far as the cooking of the meat was concerned, but the peculiar flavour of the gas was disagreeably apparent.

In fact it was to this imperfection, to overcome which the efforts of subsequent inventors were directed, that the popular prejudice against gas cooked food owed its origin. So powerful was the feeling against gas as a substitute for wood or coal in culinary operations, that eighteen years elapsed before an inventor was found sufficiently courageous to follow in the wake of Mr Hicks. This was Mr E. D. Owen who, in September 1849 patented the system which we know today, the principal feature being a hollow bulb of metal, perforated with a number of small holes.

In the following year, D. Bachoffnor, whose name is so well known in connection with earlier history of the Polytechnic Institution, and Mr N. Defries entered the field. In the system patented by these two ingenious gentlemen, a perforated pipe forming a gas-burner was fitted at the bottom of a suitable casing. Over it the meat was suspended for roasting. Above the meat were perforated shelves on which pies etc., could be baked.

Some thirty years on, Mr Thomas Fletcher, from Warrington in Lancashire, had twelve different gas cooking ranges on sale, at a cost of £7 each or £8 if the oven was lined with porcelain enamel. Not everybody approved of gas so they would bypass them and go for the Close Fire Ranges which were cheaper to run and not as complicated. Crabtrees Patent close fire would cost from £7. 15s to £14. 17s for the biggest ranges which would have two ovens and plate rack. The Kitchener had everything, baking oven, roasting oven, hot closet, gas stove, continuous plate rack hot plate, automatic cinder sifter, and ash pit. It was 60 inches wide, oven 20×23 inches, roasting oven 18×16 inches, and the hot plate was 35×16 inches—cost £21.0.0d.

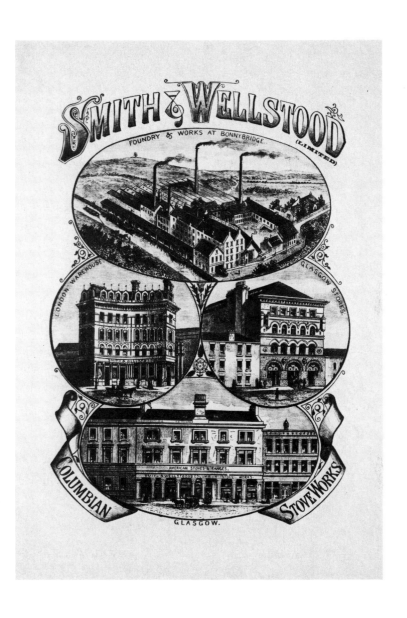

Smith and Wellstood were one of the biggest producers of
kitchen ranges in the 19th Century.

THE "LIONESS" RANGE

AT WORK.

READY FOR FRONT FIRE ROASTING, AND SHOWING THE 25 GALLON OPEN TOP COPPER HOT WATER CISTERN.

THE "ROTARY KITCHENER" STOVE.

ONE SIZE.

(top) The Mistress Range; *(bottom L)* the Lioness Range; *(bottom R)* the Rotary Kitchener Stove (invented by Dr Kitchener) (a snag was that the handle, which had to be turned in order to work the stove, would get very hot).

92

THE "NEW EMPRESS" STOVE

AS GENERALLY SET UP WHEN WITHIN THE JAMBS OF THE ORDINARY FIRE-PLACE, AND WITH 15-GALLON HOT WATER ATTACHMENT.

THIS Hot Water attachment makes a convenient and inexpensive addition, giving a ready supply of Hot Water for most of the ordinary kitchen purposes, or for a bath. It consists of a Galvanised Iron oblong Cistern, with Brass Draw-off Cock, as shown in the drawing, which rests upon an iron stand, and is screwed up to a Cast-Iron Water-Boiler or Water-Box which fits the Fire Chamber of the Stove, and is fitted to either the right side or to the left side of the Stove, as preferred. It affords a plentiful supply of Hot Water without interfering with the ordinary Cooking operations, and is easily fitted or detached.

Extra Price of same, 40/-; or if the Cistern is of Copper instead of Galvanised Iron, 50/-.

If not stated which side, the rule is to send fitted for the right-hand side, as you face the Stove; the above drawing, however, shows it on the left, the access to the Oven being on the right.

An effective heater of water (for bath or other purposes), can be fitted to and supplied with either the Nos. 8 or 9 sizes of our "NEW EMPRESS" Stove. Of heavy cast-metal, and tested to bear the pressure of two storeys height of water, it conveniently fits the Fire Chamber of the Stove, and with a little extra firing effectively serves a 25 or 30 Gallon Hot Water Tank. The "CURRENT TUBES" (flow and return) leading from this Generator pass out at either the right or left side of the Stove, as may be ordered, and are fitted with screwed nipples and nut on the outside, ready for the plumber's connections with any Tank or Cistern containing the water to be heated. The price of No. 8 Heater is £1 10/-; and No. 9, £1 15/-.

If a front Roasting Screen is required along with the other Utensils, the price of the small sized one, with stand, is 15/-; or large size, with Gibbet for a Roasting Jack, 23/-.

Smoke Pipe as required, at from 1/- to 1/6 per foot; or for the usual Closure Plate for the Throat of Chimney, and with Smoke Pipe made complete to measurement of jambs, 8/- to 10/-.

PRICES,

For Large Tinned-Iron Wash Boiler, to fit the whole Top Plate of the Stove.

| No. 6, | ... | ... | ... | ... | £0 15 0 | No. 8, | ... | ... | ... | ... | £1 0 0 |
| " 7, | ... | ... | ... | ... | 0 17 6 | " 9, | ... | ... | ... | ... | 1 5 0 |

The New Empress Stove

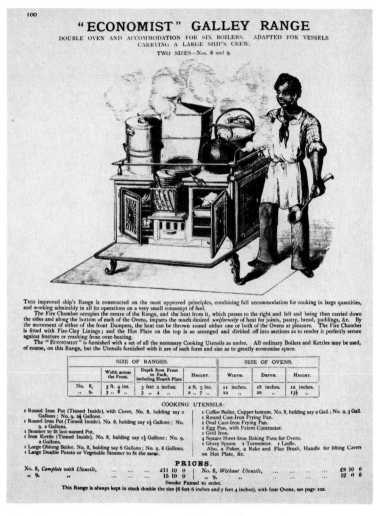

The Economist Gallery Range (this would cater for a crew of 40 — notice the bar around the edge to stop the cooking equipment moving).

Gas Cooking Stove.

Gas Cooking Stove *(Warne's)*

Both these pictures were taken at Halli'th'Wood, Bolton *(by permission of Bolton Borough Council). (top)* Crane with sliding rail for hanging skillets or a stock pot on; *(bottom)* Spit and pot crane.

A close up of the spit clock or pot crane shown in the bottom
picture on page 96.

97

IMPROVED TIN
MEAT SCREEN.

BOTTLE JACK
AND WHEEL.

Bottle jack and wheel *(Mrs Beeton)*

FRICTIONAL DAMPER

FOR FITTING INTO SHEET-IRON SMOKE PIPE.

This represents our NEW DAMPER, shown set in the pipe. By a simple arrangement, obviating the use of Springs, &c., so liable to derangement under the influence of heat, the desired purpose is admirably effected, as at any angle or position it is set the Damper is held in position by the weight of the drop handle outside.

Sizes of Damper and Prices without the Pipe.

4 ins. dia., 1/3 ; 4½ ins, 1.6 ; 5 ins., 1/9 ; 5½ and 6 ins., 2/- ; 6½ and 7 ins. 2/3.

A reduction for quantities ordered.

ARNOT'S VENTILATOR.

THE TRUE RELIABLE SELF-ACTING VENTILATOR.

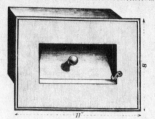

SET into the wall of the apartment opening into the Vent, as near the ceiling as possible, this Ventilator affords the surest way of carrying off impure air.

PRICE, ... 7/6.

CYLINDER SHEET-IRON COFFEE ROASTER.
THREE SIZES.

With Charcoal Furnace complete.

No. 1—Cylinder, 9 by 6 inches,	...	...	...	£0 10	0
Or with Cover,	...	...	...	0 12	6
No. 2—Cylinder, 12 by 8 inches,	...	...	...	0 12	0
Or with Cover,	...	...	...	0 15	0
No. 3—Cylinder, 15 by 10 inches,	...	...	...	0 15	0
Or with Cover,	...	...	...	0 18	6

GLOBULAR CAST-IRON COFFEE ROASTER.

ONE SIZE.

FOR USING ON A COOKING STOVE,

OR

WITH TRIVET FOR AN OPEN FIRE.

PRICE, ... 7/-

GRIP BROILER AND TOASTER.

For Broiling Steaks, Chops, or Fish, this Grilling Iron has been proved most admirable ; the juices being all saved, and the basting process self acting, the whole rich flavour is fully retained. It is made of Polished Sheet Steel. Its perforations being set up inwards prevent drip or loss of gravy into the fire. The Broiler is very light and handy in use, grips the flesh or fish firmly, and by frequent turning it distributes the gravy over the upper surface, while the under side is getting the heat, and thus imparts a uniform juiciness and tenderness to the food. This "Brander" is very suitable for use in the openings on the top of a Cooking Stove or the Hot Plate of a Close Fire Range, or over the Open Fire.

PRICES, 9 in. size, 1/6 ; 10 in. size, 2/- ; without perforations for frying pancakes, &c., 1/3 and 1/6.

WAFFLE IRON.

ONE SIZE.

FOR USING ON A COOKING STOVE OR CLOSE RANGE.

FOR BAKING BATTER-CAKES OR WAFFLES.

PRICE, ... 4/6.

Coffee roasters and toasters etc.

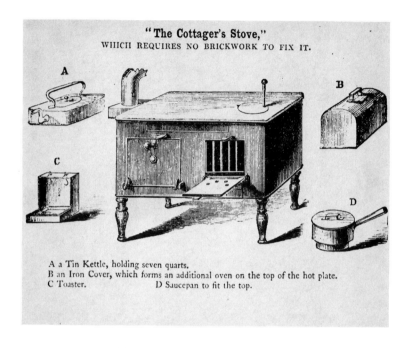

"The Cottager's Stove,"
WHICH REQUIRES NO BRICKWORK TO FIX IT.

A a Tin Kettle, holding seven quarts.
B an Iron Cover, which forms an additional oven on the top of the hot plate.
C Toaster.   D Saucepan to fit the top.

The Cottager's Stove (*Warne's*);

1860's Vegetable Cutter (*Warne's*).

A vegetable would be cut into thin slices. A slice would then be laid on the disc (chosen from one of the seven shapes) and the handle pressed down to force the vegetable through the disc.

Captain Warren's Everybody's Cooking Pot.

This new and admirable utensil we have tested ourselves, and can warmly recommend to the housekeeper. Meat is cooked in it by means of *heat only*, without being touched by any liquid, save its own juices, or even wetted by steam. The joint is put, *without water*, into the *inner* saucepan, B. This is put over the lower saucepan, A, which is filled with boiling water, the steam from which ascends round the sides of the inner pot and passes into the *lid*, which is also thus filled with steam. The meat remains cooking in its own juices alone for the period named in the following table:—

Time for Dressing Meat by Warren's Everybody's Cooking Pot.

	H.	M.
A leg of mutton, 10lbs.	3	0
Beef, 10lbs.	3	30
Goose	2	30
Turkey	3	0
Ham, 20lbs.	9	0
Hare	2	0
Rabbit	1	30

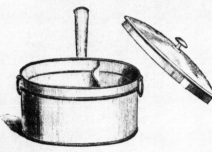

Captain Warren's Curry Pot.

Captain Warren's Everybody's Cooking Pot

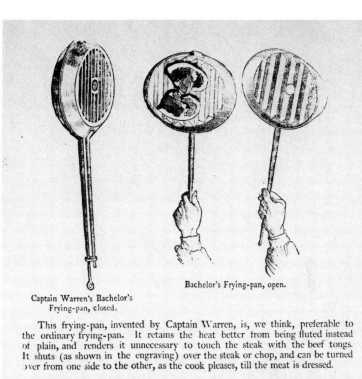

Captain Warren's Bachelor's
Frying-pan, closed.

Bachelor's Frying-pan, open.

This frying-pan, invented by Captain Warren, is, we think, preferable to the ordinary frying-pan. It retains the heat better from being fluted instead of plain, and renders it unnecessary to touch the steak with the beef tongs. It shuts (as shown in the engraving) over the steak or chop, and can be turned over from one side to the other, as the cook pleases, till the meat is dressed.

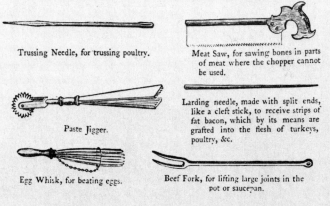

Trussing Needle, for trussing poultry.

Meat Saw, for sawing bones in parts of meat where the chopper cannot be used.

Paste Jigger.

Larding needle, made with split ends, like a cleft stick, to receive strips of fat bacon, which by its means are grafted into the flesh of turkeys, poultry, &c.

Egg Whisk, for beating eggs.

Beef Fork, for lifting large joints in the pot or saucepan.

Captain Warren's Bachelor's Frying-pan, etc. *(Warne's)*

Salmon or Jack Kettle.   Turbot Kettle.   Fish Kettle.

Saucepan.   Braising-pan.   Stewpan.

Preserving Pan, for making   Bain-marie Pan and Pots, for   Stock-pot.
jams, jellies, marmalades, &c.   keeping sauces and entrées hot, &c.

(top) Fish Kettles *(Warne's)*; *(bottom)* Pans *(Warne's)*.

104

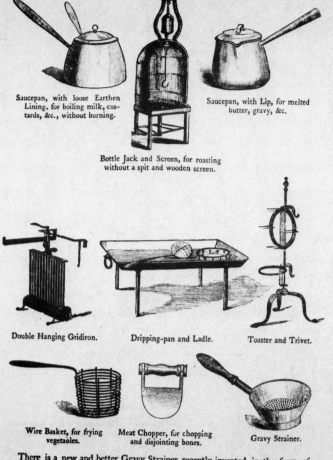

Saucepan, with loose Earthen Lining, for boiling milk, custards, &c., without burning.

Saucepan, with Lip, for melted butter, gravy, &c.

Bottle Jack and Screen, for roasting without a spit and wooden screen.

Double Hanging Gridiron.

Dripping-pan and Ladle.

Toaster and Trivet.

Wire Basket, for frying vegetables.

Meat Chopper, for chopping and disjointing bones.

Gravy Strainer.

There is a new and better Gravy Strainer recently invented, in the form of a jelly bag, perforated at the sides, which is more convenient, we think, than the ordinary one.

D

Kitchen Utensils *(Warne's)*

Pestle and Mortar.

Salamander, for browning puddings, &c.

Carson's Patent Salting Apparatus, for salting joints of meat in a few minutes.

Kent's Patent Soup Strainer.

Patent Mincing Machine.

Kent's Patent Strainer will be found most useful for procuring the transparency so much required by fashion in modern soups.

The Patent Mincing Machine will greatly economize the cook's time.

Improved Revolving Toaster, also available as a hanging Trivet, for Kettle, Saucepan, or Plate.

Egg Poacher, with a loose inside frame, and ladles to hold the eggs.

Kitchen Utensils *(Warne's)*

The cook roasting meat *(Hannah Firmin)*

Chapter 26
Meat

Carving

Carving is so important an element, both in economy and in the nice service of a meal, and is so often badly done, that it is worth while to draw your attention to a few of the principles governing it.

First you must have a really good carving knife, and see that the steel *always* has a sharp edge on it. Clean your knife yourself and sharpen it again before you put it away. I was always taught 'You look after your knives and they will look after you'.

The greatest difficulty is to hit the joints between the several bones. See also that all the skewers (if any) are drawn before you blunt your knife upon them. You should almost invariably cut across the fibres of meat, and not in the same direction. This ensures a short grain. The exception to this rule is in the case of the underside of sirloin of beef.

The next thing is to make the knife and fork help each other. The fork must steady the joint for the knife, and the knife for the fork.

Lastly, it is important to avoid waste, by cutting all slices down to the bone, so as to leave no ragged portions. We may also add that, excepting with a few joints such as mutton, slices should be thin.

For fish, silver or plated knives with wide blades so as not to break the fish unnecessarily when carving.

A larger steel knife is required for joints than for game, for which a short sharp blade is better, and a 2 pronged fork.

We cannot here enter into the methods of carving all various kinds of joints of meat, fish, poultry and game. You should see that the meats are presented well and not bitty, but sliced to a perfect thickness, ¼ inch is delicate enough and ½ inch is too much.

Whole gammon, remove the triangular section next to the knuckle end carve in a V formation along the bone taking meat from one side then the other. Carve with the knife at an oblique angle, cutting thin slices. Middle gammon is the prime cut and narrows at the bone end, so the cuts made into the jont opposite the bone should be thicker at the outside and taper towards the bone.

Rib of beef, remove the chine bone at the thick end of the joint and loosen the meat from the narrow ribs. Carve the meat in ¼ inch downward slices, serve with a thin gravy, and it should always be under cooked.

Roasting Times

Beef	15-20 minutes setting time plus 15 minutes per pound.
Lamb	15-20 minutes setting plus 20 minutes per pound.
Mutton	15 minutes setting time plus 25 minutes per pound.
Pork	25 minutes setting time plus 30 minutes per pound.
Veal	20 minutes setting time plus 25 minutes per pound.

Poultry and game are dealt with under their appropriate recipes due to their fluctuation in size.

100. Rolled Beef to Eat like Hare Warnes *Model Cookery* 1868
Time a quarter of an hour to each pound.
The *inside of a sirloin of beef, half pound of bacon, some rich gravy, two glasses of port wine, two of vinegar, twenty pound all-spice, some hare stuffing, currant jelly, and melted butter.*
Cut out the inside from a large sirloin of beef, and soak it for a day and night in a glass of port wine, and the same of vinegar; lay some good forcemeat over it, roll it, lard it, with shreds of bacon, and roast it on a hanging spit; baste it frequently with port wine and vinegar, in the same proportion that you used for soaking it; and season it with some pounded allspice. Serve it hot with a rich gravy poured around it, with currant jelly in a tureen.

101. Barbecued Pig *Young Woman's Companion* 1811
Prepare *a pig* about ten weeks old as for roasting, make forcemeat *of two anchovies six sage leaves,* and the liver of the pig, all chopped very small, then put them into a mortar, with the crumb *of half a penny loaf, 4ozs of butter, half a teaspoonful of chyan pepper, and half pint of red wine.* Beat them all together to a paste, put it in the pigs belly, and sew it up.

Lay your pig down at a good distance before a large brisk fire, singe it well, put into your dripping pan three bottles of red wine, and baste it well with this all the time it is roasting. When it is half done, put under the pig two penny loaves, and if you find your wine too much reduced, add more.

When your pig is near enough, take the loaves and sauce out of your dripping-pan, and put to the sauce *one anchovy* chopped small, *a bundle of sweet herbs, and half a lemon.* Boil it a few minutes, then draw your pig, put a *small lemon or apple* in the pigs mouth, and a *leaf* on each side. Strain your sauce, and pour it on boiling hot. Send it up to the table garnished with barberries and sliced lemon.

102. Barbecued Pork

I am a great lover of barbecued food, that being the modern version of barbecuing Chinese or American style, though the recipe I am giving you for barbecued pork is an Italian recipe from a restaurateur called Pino, who had a restaurant in Wilmslow, Cheshire called Pino's Quo-Vadis.

The first thing we make is the sauce for which we will require: *¾lb butter, 1 large chopped onion, 3 garlic cloves chopped very fine, 5ozs tomato puree, 7ozs brown sugar, 1 teaspoon of salt, 1 teaspoon of freshly ground pepper, the juice of 1 lemon, 1½ tablespoons of crushed fennel seed, 3 bay leaves, ¾ teaspoon of tabasco, 1 teaspoon of basil, and 4 ozs of fresh honey, 2 pints of stock.*

Put the above sauce ingredients into a large baking tray and boil for 15 minutes. Place *2lb of pork fillets* in the marinade for 24 hours, then cook slowly in a low oven for 2 hours. Take out the port fillets and thicken the sauce with *cornflour*. Pour the now thick sauce over the pork and serve.

103. Leg of Mutton a la haute gout *Young Womans Companion* 1811

Take a *fine leg of mutton* that has hung a fortnight (if the weather will permit) and stuff every part of it with some *cloves of garlic,* rub it with *pepper and salt,* and then roast it. When it is properly done, send it up with some good gravy and red wine in the dish. Garnish with pickles and barberries.

104. A shoulder of Mutton called Hen and Chickens. *Frugal Housewife* 1829

This is a very unusual dish for this period, notice that cayenne is spelt chyan and green pickles were used for the garnish.

Half roast a shoulder of mutton then take it up, and cut off the blade at the first joint, and both the flaps to make the blade round; score the blade round in diamonds, throw a *little pepper and salt* over it, and set it in a tin oven to broil. Cut the flaps and meat off the shank in thin slices, and put the gravy that came out of the mutton into a stewpan, with *a little good gravy, two spoonfuls of walnut catchup, one of browning, a little chyan pepper, and one or two shallots.*

When your meat is tender, thicken it with *flour and butter,* put it into the dish with the gravy and lay the blade on the top. Garnish with green pickles.

105. Curing Hams the Yorkshire Way (1868)

Mix well together *half a peck of salt, three ounces of salt petre, half an ounce of sal-prunella, and five pounds of very coarse salt.* Rub the hams well with this, put them into a large pan or pickling tub and lay the remainder on the top. Let them lay three days and then hang them up. Put as much water to the pickle as will cover the hams adding salt. It will bear an egg, and then boil and strain it. The next morning put in the hams and press them down so that they may be covered. Let them lay a fortnight then rub them well with bran and dry them. The quantity of ingredients here directed is for doing three middle sized hams at once, so that if you do only one you must proportion the quantity of each article.

106. Curing Hams the Yorkshire Way (Author's recipe)

Today all we need to do is let them soak for 24 hours changing the water after 12 hours, clean and trim, and put it in a large saucepan cooking it gently for 35 minutes per pound.

When cooked remove the ham, strip off the skin, cover with *honey,* and stick *cloves* into the ham, at every inch square. Cook slowly in the oven Gas 3 325F for ¾ hour. Let it cool and serve with salad or cabbage and new potatoes.

107. Shoulder of Veal a la Piedmontoise (1811)

Cut the skin off *a shoulder of veal,* so that it may hang at one end; then lard the meat with *bacon or ham* and season it with *pepper, salt, mace, sweet herbs, parsley and lemon peel.* Cover it again with the skin, stew it with gravy and when it is tender take it up. Then take *sorrel, some lettuce chopped small* and stew them in some butter with *parsley, onions and mushrooms.* When the herbs are tender put to them some of the liquor, some *sweetbreads and bits of ham.* Let all stew together a short time then lift up the skin, moisten it with *melted butter,* strew over it *crumbs of bread* and send it to the oven to brown. Serve it up hot with some good gravy in the dish.

Chapter 27
The Victorian Servant

The Victorian age brought more servants into the households of the gentry. Girls and boys from all over the country who had no trades went into service. They knew nothing about cooking, so more and more cookery books were being brought into the households.

The ordinary middle class household, unlike the great kitchen and the fifteen chefs Careme had under him, consisted of a cook, upper housemaid, nursemaid, under housemaid, general servant, and footboy, which in 1837, the beginning of the reign of Queen Victoria, cost £600 a year; to have six servants you had to have a good income.

An under-housemaid would get less than £80 a year, but had a job of honour, and would work an 18 hour day, with 3 meals a day, and a bed to sleep in. That was luxury for any servant.

The general servant had to be up very early to open all the shutters around the house. She would then have the kitchen range to clean and polish before the cook got up. If this was not done properly she would forgo luxuries such as fruit, cakes or home-made lemonade, which was always a refreshing favourite of the downstairs staff.

After cleaning the cooker, it was into the breakfast room, to remove the fender, clean the grate and light the fire. After about 5 minutes, when the dust had settled in that now warm breakfast room she would return to dust, before laying out the breakfast. With one hour before the breakfast bell is rung it's time to sweep the hall, shake the mats, clean the doorstep and polish the brass on the door (I'm tired already). Now it's time to clean the boots of the household which would consist of about 10 pairs. Five minutes to go before breakfast for the household.

The servant, Marie as we will call her in future, would now wash her hands and face and change her apron. The toast would then be cooked over the fire she had made in the kitchen and also the kippers, eggs, bacon and kidneys etc. Marie would then have her own breakfast, if the cooking range was clean enough! Beds have now to be stripped down and all windows opened. And the wonder of inventions, the chamber-pots to be emptied.

The bell would ring and it is now time to clear off the breakfast

Peeling potatoes *(Hannah Firmin)*

113

table and rekindle the fire. The stairs and bannisters need sweeping and dusting. After cleaning the drawing room little Marie can now start to peel the vegetables for lunch. Half an hour before lunch she would lay the cloth and put the bread on the bread board and set the cutlery out. When lunch is finished she would have a kettle of boiling water ready, for the dishes to be washed.

She then cleans up the kitchen and prepares for dinner. At her leisure she works at her needle, and keeps the linen in good repair.

I have a very amusing extract here from a book called *Dinners and Dinner Parties* in 1862 by G.V. He was a man with a great sense of humour. I hope you enjoy this as I did.

G.V. 1862 *Dinners and Dinner Parties*

To the Reader

The Three Million Seven Hundred and Forty Five Thousand Four Hundred and Sixty Three Housewives of England and Wales may read this book to their improvement, and although there are statements that may cause them to blush, there is nothing but what their daughters may read.

The yachtsmen, the sportsmen and the bachelors will find many rules for creature comforts, and will learn how to avoid the evils that destroy the pleasures of life and send them early to eternity.

The Legislature will find suggestions worthy of attention, although it may not think proper to return to the penalties of the statute of 22 Henry VIII, under which two cooks-viz. John Roose and Margaret Davy — were boiled to death.

The impostor dinner-givers have not been forgotten, their dinners and guests are described, their servants portrayed and their hospitality commented on.

The dame of the man of independence should be proud of her position; she should try and remedy the evil that drives her husband to his club. If she be unable to give instructions, or be unable to read a cookery book let her employ some one above the woman she employs to clean her street-doorsteps-a woman born in a shed, or under the lee of a brick-kiln, who most probably never tasted meat in the hole from whence she came. Common sense dictates that such a person ought not to be entrusted to cook anything beyond what is fitted for the pigsty. At all events, every cook should be educated so as to be able to read a book on cookery and instead of being at the bottom of the ladder, should take her place as the first person in the household.

The author was present with a young lady who had been educated in the usual nonsense, when the footman entered and asked her mother if he could say a word to her in private; the mother answered that she wished no secrets, and desired him to speak out; he hesitating, she bid him to say what he had to say.

He replied, "I think it right to tell you, mam, that cook was drunk last night, and, in pouring out the soup from the saucepan into the tureen, was ill, and before she could turn her head away from it, part of her illness went into the tureen". Cook was immediately called up, but of course, the brute stoutly denied it. However, there was no doubt of the fact; the footman said he did not like to disturb the party, so he wiped the edge of the tureen, and gave the soup a good stir. The lady, in great anguish, exclaimed, "Good Heavens! I ate some of it!" and, being highly indignant, was not very gentle either to William for stirring the soup, or the cook for her addition to it. The young lady listlessly exclaimed, "I ate some of it; but what a fuss you are making, mamma! You know we must all eat a peck of dirt before we die".

Great excuse may be made for the women of England of the present century in the fact that they have never been instructed, but, on the contrary, taught to consider their household duties as an offensive occupation. The kitchens, for the most part, are dark and underground, the iron utensils generally furnished are black and dirty, not fit to be handled any more than they are fitted for the purpose they are used.

The cooks are the sisters or cousins of the recruits of our army, who are paid one shilling per day, and no more, from which sevenpence is taken for their food.

G.V. then goes on about how people should be educated on food in the workhouses and schools, and diplomas should be granted by the Educational Council:—

There are few housewives that know anything at all of domestic duty, and there are no female servants of character fitted for the duties, although the females above 21 years of age number 600,000 more than the male (1860) population, but not one in a hundred knows how to cook a potato.

There is scarcely an individual in the United Kingdom that is not the victim to dyspepsia, and consequently, to misery and premature death, because the deputies that are appointed by the housewives are wholly incompetent to prepare any food, even for a hog. How can it be otherwise? They are taken from the very dregs of society, out of hovels and rookeries, probably from the workhouse. It is notorious that when these creatures enter your kitchen they know not the purpose of the different utensils, which they always misuse. These are not the class of women that are required; they are dirty in the extreme, and know not what cleanliness means. Wives may think cleanliness in a cook of no importance, but the chemist would tell her that food should be chemically clean, or it is changed in character, and rendered unfit for the human stomach; and as to children, he would tell her that millions have been diseased for life, and millions have been killed in infancy, by dirty and improperly prepared food.

Not one in ten of the persons that go out as domestic servants knows her alphabet, and not one in twenty can read a book on cookery so as to understand it, but what they lack in reading they make up in impudence — sheer impudence; they are largely gifted with that commodity called brass, and will tell a lie and stick to it; they are artful and full of low cunning; and know that their mistresses are frightened, and at their mercy. Nearly every cook disputes the right of her mistress to enter her kitchen, and many a mistress has conceded the point for peace' sake, and tried to coax the creature into good humour, although she knew her to be a thief.

Chapter 28
Vegetables

We must not forget, while enjoying the cookery of the past, that every age and every country have been laid under contribution to supply the materials with which the modern cooks and chefs work.

Asparagus, horseradish, cabbage, turnips, carrots and parsnips are native vegetables, but we owe the bean to the Romans. The scarlet-runner came from South America in 1633; Peas came from the south of Europe in Henry VIII's reign.

The cauliflower came from Cyprus in 1694; the potato we owe to South America and again the Jerusalem artichoke came from Brazil in 1716; red beetroot was introduced from the south of Europe in 1656; the radish is a native of China and Japan, and was introduced around 1584; Japan sent the onion (1859), onions are co-eval with the mysteries of ancient Egypt; the leek came from Switzerland, the shallot comes from Palestine and parsley is from Sardinia.

We owe to many lands and many ages the daily, and too little valued, delicacies of our table.

As a race I am afraid we still do not make the best of our vegetables. Food experts even go so far as to say we should be more sensible if, instead of serving up the vegetables and throwing away the water, we were to keep the water and let the vegetables go. One can put it in a few words. Never overcook vegetables. If you boil them put them in the minimum of water and do not let it go off the boil. Do not use soda to preserve the colour. A pinch of sugar does just as well, and does not make vegetables indigestible as soda is said to do, nor does it destroy their vitamins. Cooking makes many vegetables more palatable and more digestible, my golden rule for anyone cooking vegetables is always undercook them (eldente), always wash them off in cold water if you are not serving them up straight away. Do not reboil them. Bring a pan of hot salted water to the boil and drop them in for a few minutes, or toss them in hot butter with ground pepper and salt.

Rosa Lewis had an obsession about vegetables, she would cook the potatoes, asparagus and beans herself, she would not give them to the scullery maid — or person without brain as she put it — because they were more expensive than the meat, and more essential than anything else in the dinner.

Colour in food for presentation is essential. It was not a rule until mid-nineteenth century, that vegetables were treated with care. I agree with Rosa Lewis that if the vegetables are not treated with respect then the complete meal would be let down.

Vegetables from *The Young Woman's Companion* 1811.

In dressing these articles the greatest attention must be paid to cleanliness. They are particularly at some times of the year subject to dust, dirt and insects, so that if they are not properly cleansed, they will be unsatisfactory to those for whom they are provided, and disreputable to the cook.

To avoid this, be careful first to pick off all the outside leaves, then wash them well in several waters, and let them lay some time in a pan of clean water before you dress them. Be sure your saucepan is thoroughly clean, and boil them by themselves in plenty of water. They should always be brought crisp to the table, which will be effected by being careful not to boil them too much.

Such are the general observations neccessary to be attended to in dressing vegetables. We shall now proceed to particulars begining with:—

108. Asparagus (1811)
Scrape all the stalks very carefully till they look white, then cut them all even alike and throw them into a pan of clean water, and have ready a stewpan with boiling water. Put some *salt* in and tie the asparagus in little bunches, put them in and when they are a little tender, take them out.

If you boil them too much, they will lose both their colour and taste. Cut the round off *a small loaf,* about half an inch thick and toast it brown on both sides: then dip it into the liquor the asparagus was boiled in, and lay it in your dish. Pour *a little melted butter* over your toast and then your asparagus (not too much on the asparagus), send it to the table with melted butter in a basin.

109. Artichokes (1805)
Twist off the stalks, then put them into cold water and wash them well. When the water boils, put them in with the tops downwards, that all the dust and sand may boil out. About an hour and a half or two hours will do them. Serve them up with *melted butter* in cups.

110. Artichokes *Domestic Cookery* (1843)

Twist off the stalks then put them into cold water and wash them well. When the water boils put them in with the tops downwards, that all the dust and sand may boil out. About an hour and a half, or two hours will do them. Serve them up with *melted butter* in cups.

Notice the time element between the above and the recipe 20 years later, and the difference in methods.

111. Artichokes *Warnes* (1868)

Two tablespoonfuls of salt and a piece of soda the size of a sixpenny to every gallon of water.

Gather the artichokes two or three days before they are required for use. Cut off the stems, pull out the strings, and wash them in two or three waters that no insects may be in them. Have a large pan of boiling water with the above quantities of soda and salt.

Put the artichokes with the tops downwards and let them boil quickly until tender about a half hour, but that can be ascertained by pulling out one of the leaves; (if they come out easily they are done, I would give it another 15 minutes). Take them out, and lay them on a napkin, with *a tureen of melted butter,* allowing a teacupful to each artichoke.

They may be served without a napkin on a hot dish, with white sauce poured over them.

112. To Dress Dandelions like Spinach: Eliza Acton (1845)

This common weed of the fields and highways, is an excellent vegetable, the young leaves forming an admirable adjunct to salad, and much resembling endive when boiled and prepared in the same way, or in any modes directed for spinach. The slight bitterness of its flavour is to many persons very agreeable; and it is often served at well appointed tables. It has also, we believe, the advantage of possessing valuable medicinal qualities. Take the roots before the blossom is at all advanced, if they can readily be found in that state; if not pluck off and use the young leaves only. Wash them as clean as possible, and boil them tender in a large quantity of water salted as for sprouts or spinach. Drain them well, press them dry with a wooden spoon, and serve them quite plain with melted butter in a tureen; or squeeze, chop and heat them afresh, with a seasoning of *salt and pepper, a morsel of butter rolled in flour, and a spoonful or two of gravy or cream.*

A very large portion of the leaves will be required for a dish, as they shrink exceedingly in the cooking. For a salad, take them very young and serve them entire, or break them quite small with the fingers; then wash and drain them. Dress them with oil and vinegar, or with any other sauce which may be preferred with them.

113. Parsnips
These must be boiled in plenty of water, and when they are soft, which you may know by running a fork into them take them up. Scrape them all fine with a knife, throw away all the sticky part, and send them to table, with melted butter in a sauce boat.

Mushrooms are best when small and freshly picked (buttons). They are white or brownish in colour, with pink gills darkening to colour almost black, and should have firm, brittle flesh, and ought not to change colour when cut. The common mushroom found in our pastures is the *agaricus campestris.*

Never chance eating mushrooms that are wild at all, unless you do know a great deal about them. Excellent for salads, soups, baked or grilled.

114. Stuffed Mushrooms
1 cupful of mushrooms, chopped ham, breadcrumbs, 1 teaspoonful of chopped spring onions, pepper and salt, a little milk or stock, croutons of fried bread, and some tartar sauce, and chopped parsley.

Prepare the fried croutons and keep them hot. Wash the mushrooms, remove the stalks. Chop up the ham. Mix together the ham, breadcrumbs, parsley, and seasoning, bind with a little milk or stock. Fill the mushrooms with this mixture, put a small piece of butter on each mushroom, and fry slowly for 10 minutes. Lay each one on a crouton, pour the butter over them, place some tartar sauce and parsley on the side and serve. This makes an excellent starter for an evening meal.

115. Mushroom Souffle
2ozs butter, 2ozs flour, ½ pint of milk, 8ozs mushrooms, 6 eggs, salt and ground black pepper, with a teaspoon of Watkins Mushroom Ketchup.

Melt the butter in a saucepan, stir in the flour and cook for 5 minutes, stirring in the mushroom ketchup. Gradually add the milk, bring to the boil and cook until it is thick and creamy. Add the finely chopped mushrooms. Now separate the yolks from the white of the eggs, add them with the salt and pepper to taste. Cook slowly for 1 minute while you whisk your egg white stiff, folding them in slowly. Put the mixture into a well greased souffle dish. Bake in an oven for 30 minutes Gas 5, 375F in the centre of the oven.

Chapter 29
Herbs

In the 1800's if you were ill and could not eat you would go to your Doctor if you had the money, but as they were far too expensive, for the majority of people they became their own physicians. By using nature's remedies the herbalist became more popular than any doctor.

The herbalist, in presenting his work of crude organic remedies made his objective to present new and curious, if not startling, facts not only well worthy of the earnest consideration of the more intelligent portion of the community but also as a good way of making money. A herbalist was never seen to be poor. Some of the nineteenth century herbal remedies are given in the next chapter. Here are some of the herbs used for those Victorian recipes and some of their other uses:-

Herbs and Spices and their uses

Herb	*Uses*
Allspice	Whole in meat and fish dishes. Ground in pickles, cakes, milk puddings and fruit pies.
Angelica	These can be candied and used for flavouring and decorating cakes, sweets and fruits.
Aniseed	Salad dressings, flavouring drinks, the leaves for soups and sweets.
Balm	Flavouring soups, stews, sauces and dressings.
Basil	Tomato dishes, soups and sauces, lamb dishes and salads.
Bay leaves	One of the most popular herbs
Borage	Use in salads, shoots are used in fruit cups and drinks.
Caraway Seed	In bread, cheese spreads, pickles, cakes, soups and sauces.
Cardamom	In pickles, curries, bread, biscuits and cakes.
Celery seed	Combined with salt you have celery salt, on its own can be used in barbecue sauces, pickles and salad dressings.
Chervil	As a garnish in salads, very similar to parsley.

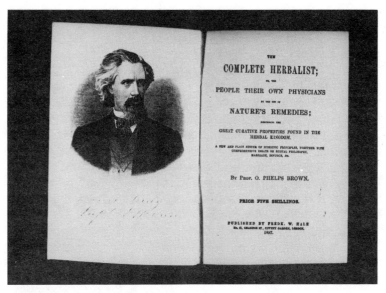

THE
COMPLETE HERBALIST;

PEOPLE THEIR OWN PHYSICIANS

NATURE'S REMEDIES;

GREAT CURATIVE PROPERTIES FOUND IN THE
HERBAL KINGDOM.

A NEW AND PLAIN SYSTEM OF HYGIENIC PRINCIPLES, TOGETHER WITH
COMPREHENSIVE ESSAYS ON SEXUAL PHILOSOPHY,
MARRIAGE, DIVORCE, &c.

By Prof. O. PHELPS BROWN.

PRICE FIVE SHILLINGS.

PUBLISHED BY FREDK. W. HALE
No. 6, CHANDOS ST., COVENT GARDEN, LONDON,
1897.

Yellow Parilla.   Atropa Mandragora.

(top) The Complete Herbalist by Professor O. Phelps Brown
(1897); *(bottom L)* Yellow Parilla, commonly known as the Vine-
Maple and used by the Victorians as a tonic and laxative;
(bottom R) Atropa Mandragora, commonly known as the
Mandrake, very poisonous and repulsive to taste. Both herbs and
that on the next page are from the above book.

121

Helleborus Niger.

(top L) Helleborus Niger, commonly known as Henbane and a powerful narcotic; *(top R)* Pestle and mortar, used mainly for grinding seed herbs and blending *(by permission of Bolton Borough Council)*; *(bottom)* Oak spice and herb box *(by permission of Bolton Borough Council)*.

Stock Pot, made of gun metal in the late 17th Century. This
would be on the go twenty-four hours a day, with carcasses,
vegetables and herbs *(by permission of Bolton Borough Council)*.

Herb	Uses
Chives	Use wherever onion flavour is wanted, in soups, omelettes, salads and entrees.
Chilli powder	Blend of Spices with chilli pepper as the basic ingredients used in meat dishes, sauces, seafood, curries and cocktail dips.
Coriander	In pickles or for flavouring cakes, sauces and drinks
Cinnamon	Reddish brown sticks for preserving and mulled wines. Used ground in cakes, milk puddings and in fruit pies, e.g. apple.
Cloves	An excellent seasoning for both savoury and sweet dishes, it has a strong flavour so use sparingly. Use whole to stud roast ham or pork and ground in milk pudding, Christmas pudding and biscuits.
Cumin	One of the main ingredients in curry powder, often used in Mexican, Indian and Spanish meat dishes.
Curry Powder	This is a blend of many spices and used in all dishes hot and cold.
Dill	Similar to caraway, can be used as a garnish for salads and seafood dishes, flavouring for soups, sauces and in preserves or pickle.
Fennel	A herb I myself would never be without, it has a sweet aniseed flavour used mostly in sauces.
Garlic	In salads or for flavouring all foods.
Ginger	The Chinese use this a great deal in their cookery, we use it in cakes, biscuits, on melon, in curries and sauces.
Horseradish	Flavouring sauces or shredded in a salad.
Hyssop	Flavouring soups and in the distillation of liqueurs.
Mace	Whole in pickles and preserves, ground in fish, meat and cheese dishes very much like nutmeg.
Marjoram	In stuffings, soups and Italian dishes.
Mint	Mint sauce or jelly, flavouring sauces, soups or vegetables.
Mustard Seed	Brown or yellow seed, often used for condiments for meat.
Nutmeg	Milk puddings, soups, custards and vegetables.

Herb	Uses
Oregano	Used in Greek, Mexican and Italian dishes, mostly salad dressings and egg dishes.
Parsley	As a garnish, for flavouring soups and sauces.
Paprika	Meat, poultry, cheese dishes, salads, and a garnish for salads, egg and soup dishes.
Pepper	Whole black and white peppercorns, used in most main dishes
Poppy seed	Mainly used in baking pastries, bread and a garnish for snack and cheese dishes.
Purslane	Salads, flavouring soups and sauces.
Rosemary	In salads or for flavouring stews, sauces and lamb dishes.
Rue	Flavouring fruit cups.
Sage	In stuffings, soups, sauces, mainly pork and poultry.
Savory	In egg dishes, as a garnish, in stuffings, or for flavouring soups and sauces.
Sesame	Sprinkled on bread, biscuits and cakes before cooking.
Sorrel	In salads, or flavouring soups and as a vegetable.
Southernwood	Flavouring cakes.
Tansy	Garnish in salads for flavouring puddings, cakes and stews.
Tarragon	In sauces, salads, for making tarragon vinegar.
Thyme	In stuffings or for flavouring soups, stews, meat and poultry dishes.
Turmeric	Related to ginger, another essential ingredient of curry powder, used in mustard, and colouring cakes and rice.
Violet	Their petals are candied in sugar, and can be used in salads for aroma.

Chapter 30
Herbal Remedies (1840)

The following are 1840 herbal remedies. The modern reader should take medical advice before relying on them.

116. Barley Water
Pearl Barley, two ounces, boiling water, two quarts.
Boil to one quart and strain. If desirable a little *lemon juice and sugar* can be added. This may be taken freely for all inflammatory and eruptive diseases: Measles, Scarlet Fever, Smallpox, etc.

117. Isinglass Jelly
Isinglass, two ounces, water, two pints.
Boil to one pint. Strain and add *one pint of milk and one ounce of white sugar*. This is excellent for persons recovering from sickness and children who have bowel complaints.

118. Rice
In all cases where a light and nice diet for parties who have been or are afflicted with diarrhoea or dysentery is required, rice, in almost any cooked form is most agreeable and advantageous. It may be given with benefit to dyspepsics, unless costiveness accompanies the dysentery.

119. Arrowroot Gruel
Arrowroot, one tablespoonful, sweet milk and boiling water, each one half pint.
Sweeten with *sugar loaf.* This is very good for children whose bowels are irritable.

120. Drink in Dysentery
Sheeps suet, two ounces, milk, one pint, starch, half an ounce.
Boil gently for thirty minutes. Use as a common drink. This is excellent in sustaining the strength in bad cases of dysentery.

121. Mustard Whey
Bruised mustard seed, two tablespoons; milk, one quart.
Boil together for a few minutes until it coagulates and strain to separate the curd. This is a very useful drink in dropsy. A teacupful may be taken as a dose, three times a day.

122. Slippery Elm Jelly

Take of *the flour of slippery elm one or two teaspoonfuls; cold water, one pint.* Stir until a jelly is formed. Sweeten with *loaf sugar or honey.* This is excellent for all diseases of the throat, chest and lungs, coughs, colds, bronchitis, inflammation of the lungs, etc. It is very nutritious and soothing.

123. Malt Infusion

Infuse *one pint of ground malt,* for two hours, in *three pints of scalding water.* The water should not be brought quite to the boiling point. Strain, *add sugar* if desired; flavour with *lemon juice.* This is an excellent drink in inflammatory fevers, acute rheumatism, etc.

124. Water Gruel

Corn or oatmeal, two tablespoonfuls; water, one quart.
Boil ten or fifteen minutes and strain. Add *salt and sugar* to suit the taste of the patient. This should be used freely during and after the operation of cathartic medicines.

125. Beef Tea

Cut *one pound of lean beef* into shreds and boil for twenty minutes in one *quart of water,* being particular to remove the scum as often as it arises. When it is cool, strain. This is very nourishing and palatable, and is of great value in cases of extreme debility, where no inflammatory action exists, or after the inflammation is subdued. In very low cases a small teaspoonful may be administered every fifteen or twenty minutes, gradually increasing the amount given as the powers of life return.

Chapter 31
Health Foods

Nature's Food for Slimmers 1890

Our aim should be to eat only when we are hungry, and drink when we are thirsty. To do this we must live as close to Nature as possible, and rule out all stimulating foods and drinks.

Three light meals per day are sufficient for most people, and many would be wise to take nothing but a fruit breakfast.

Liquids should be taken between meals, or else sipped slowly at the end of meals.

Strong tea and coffee are harmful stimulants. It is better to take weak China tea, fig or dandelion coffee.

Nature's health foods (author)

Apple

The king of the fruits, being the most important in temperate zones. British apples are unrivalled for their flavour and richness in organic salts. The apple contains sodium potassium and malic acid. Best apples to grow are Cox's Orange Pippin.

Barley

Avoid pearl barley which has been robbed of its mineral salts, and eat only pot or whole barley. Being deficient in gluten barley does not make good bread, but barley meal or flour does and also makes delicious scones. Barley is rich in magnesium, and is a good food for athletes.

Blackberries

The blackberry or bramble makes a good preserve, but is best eaten raw or ripe like all other fruits. It can be improved by cultivation, and is rich in natural sugar, lime and magnesium.

Blackcurrants

Fresh raw blackcurrants are exceedingly rich in antiscorbutic acid, and a drink made from sweetened juice may contain as much as five times the vitamin C content as is found in the same amount of orange juice. Blackcurrant jam retains some vitamin C, and canned or bottled fruit heated in a vacuum is almost as good as the fresh fruit. Redcurrants are also rich in vitamin C and contain both malic and citric acid.

Celery
This wholesome vegetable has a very high sodium content, hence is useful in rheumatism and all acid troubles. It belongs to the parsley family and is a splendid alkaline food.

Chive
A small bulbous plant belonging to the onion family. Can be propagated simply by dividing the root. Gives an excellent flavour to salads and is a stimulant of digestive juices. Rich in lime, sulphur and potassium.

Corn Salad
This native wild plant makes an excellent ingredient of the salad dish and may be used in winter and spring when lettuces are scarce or not to the usual standards. I myself also use chinese leaves which, like corn salad, are rich in vitamins and sodium, the positive tissue salt.

Dandelion
These young crisp leaves are very good for salads and are rich organic mineral salts. They contain also most of the essential vitamins. They are good for skin troubles and all affections of the liver. A very under-rated plant, which we today do not use to our full advantage, when you consider you can walk in any field and pick them for nothing in England.

Garlic
Although some people cannot tolerate it, this plant is very valuable as a cleansing and disinfectant agent. It is also called "poor man's theriac." Aristophanes wrote that athletes used to eat it before doing their exercises in the stadium. I use it a great deal in my salads. Contains iodine and sulphur, and I have not seen a vampire yet.

Kail
A hardy species of the cabbage with finely curled leaves. Stands the winter well and can be used as a spring vegetable. Rich in alkaline minerals and a good cleansing food. I remember collecting it myself when I was thirteen and eating it raw and I was told by a chef called Eric Shaw that it would make my hair curl if I rubbed my hair with it, now I am nearly bald.

Lettuce
There are two main types — cabbage and cos, the web being my favourite, being the best all round salad plant. It is rich in most

vitamins, iron, sodium and lime. The dark outer leaves are the richest in nutritive value. Can be grown "all year round", the latter being a splendid kind to cultivate.

Oats
Our richest cereal in fats and mineral salts. A splendid body-building food, and excellent for growing children. As it contains an alkaloid called avenin, oatmeal has a heating effect on the blood, and so the daily diet should contain plenty of greenstuff like lettuce or kail. Oatmeal is best eaten in the form of oatcakes or bannocks.

Parsley
A highly esteemed plant rich in vitamins and a diuretic oil good for liver and kidney troubles. The plain-leaved variety stands the winter best.

Pears
The same family as the apple, but more difficult to cultivate. Conference is the best self-fertile variety. Pears contain more sugar and less malic acid than apples.

Plum
A hardy native fruit which is getting more popular in the British restaurants, I like Victoria, the most reliable kind, and ripe fruit is rich in sugar and mineral salts, very good blood purifiers.

Potato
The Golden Wonder, Maris Piper and the King Edward are the most popular. Potatoes contain easily digested starch and valuable alkaline salts.

Raspberry
One of the best summer fruits and is easily grown. Lloyd George is a reliable cropper. The ripe berries contain sugar, small amount of protein and some malic acid.

Rice
The staple food of the East, and is not so nourishing as wheat or oatmeal. Only the natural brown or unpolished rice should be used. Rice is rich in sodium and is good for kidney troubles and Uncle Ben.

Spinach
Excellent alkaline salad for health purposes. Rich in iron and vitamins. Good for gland troubles. Best spinach is best for winter growth.

Strawberries

The most popular fruit of the summer here in England and a chef's delight when it comes to making sweets. A well-flavoured berry of great hygienic value. Rich in organic salts and iron. Good for rheumatism and acid complaints (deficiencies).

Tomato

Our richest food plant in vitamins A, B and C. Contains malic and trace oxalic acid. Also lime, potash and iron. Excellent for liver troubles.

Wheat

The milling away of the bran, germ and mineral salts is responsible to-day for the awful prevalence of constipation and most of our deficiency diseases. Wholemeal bread made from 100% of the wheat berry is the best that money can buy. Wholemeal biscuits are good for the teeth and bone tissues. Rich in vitamin B.

Chapter 32
Vegetarian Dishes and Savouries

Vegetarian dishes were a great help in solving the problem of what to eat, whether you were a vegetarian or not in the 19th century. If you could not afford meat then you would have a cheap substitute. Not until the middle of the century was pasta introduced, then it was not very popular. In the middle class household it was classed as a second course dish, and the poor families would eat it raw, or make a broth of it. We did learn a lot from the eating habits of vegetarians. Eggs, milk, macaroni, semolina and all vegetables are the main diet, and they will always under cook their vegetables. I will also include spaghetti in the savouries even though you would never find spaghetti in a 19th century cookbook.

One does not have to be a vegetarian to enjoy non-meat dishes. You will find that vegetarian cookery stimulates your imagination to help you produce more interesting vegetable side dishes, excellent starters and a little more excitement into cooking.

126. Cheese Pudding
2ozs grated cheese, 1 egg, 1oz butter, 2ozs breadcrumbs, ½ pint of milk and a little English mustard, salt and pepper to taste.
Heat the milk and stir in the butter, breadcrumbs, mustard and salt, and add the cheese and the beaten egg yolk. Whip the white to a stiff froth and fold in very lightly. Pour the mixture into a greased pie dish and bake for 20 minutes.

127. Lentil Cutlets
2ozs mashed potaotes, 1 egg, stick of celery, 1 carrot diced, 1 onion, ½lb red lentils, salt and pepper to taste, flour and breadcrumbs.
Soak the lentils for 3 hours. Cook them until they are soft, with the onion, carrot, celery all chopped very fine and enough water to cover. Then put them through a fine sieve. Add the puree to the potatoes, seasoning and a little butter. Add the egg to bond. Allow the mixture to cool, and form them into cutlet shapes, flour and breadcrumb them and cook in butter until golden brown.

128. Macaroni Cheese

½lb macaroni, 8ozs grated cheese, 2ozs butter, ½ pint of milk, salt and pepper.

Put the macaroni into boiling salted water and cook until tender. Drain it well and put it into a fireproof dish with layers of grated cheese, seasoning each layer. Add the milk, and sprinkle the grated cheese on top. Put a few lumps of butter on this. Bake in the oven for 25 minutes until golden brown.

129. Marco Polo's Pie

Marco Polo, was introduced into Italy after the great man came back from China in 1295 with his introduction of pasta. So they named this beautiful pie after him.

Make enough *pastry for a 9 inch pie dish, 1 onion chopped, 1 carrot chopped, 8ozs cooked macaroni, 8ozs cooked spinach, 4 egg yolks, 4ozs grated cheese, 1lb of tomatoes (peeled and chopped), 1 pinch of thyme, 1 crumbled bay leaf, ¾lb of chopped mushrooms, ¼ pint of double cream, salt and freshly ground black pepper.*

Saute off in a frying pan the onions, carrots and mushrooms, then blend together all the other ingredients. Put the pastry base in the dish, place all the ingredients in, put on top, and bake in a pre-heated oven for 35 minutes gas 6.

Rice dishes are also popular with vegetarians, the most popular dish being a Risotto. I use the best long grain rice for all my rice dishes and suggest you do the same.

130. Country Style Risotto

1 small onion chopped, 2 large courgettes sliced, 2 small zucchini sliced, ¾lb peas, 12 cooked asparagus tips, 6 large tomatoes peeled and sliced, ¼lb cooked green beans, 1lb cooked rice, 2ozs best butter, 1 clove of garlic, salt and ground black pepper, vegetable broth (1 pint) and 3 tablespoons of olive oil.

Saute the onion in 3 tablespoons of olive oil until transparent. Add the peas and zucchini and cook for 1 minute, add the green beans and courgettes. Add some vegetable broth to completely cover. Cook for a further 8 minutes, add tomatoes, garlic, salt and pepper, simmer for another 12 minutes. Stir in the rice and add enough broth and simmer for a further 12 minutes or until the liquid is absorbed. Add the butter and asparagus, let them blend for a minute, place into a large dish garnished with hard boiled eggs.

131. Spaghetti in Cream Sauce

1lb spaghetti, 1 clove of garlic, 2 tablespoons of olive oil, 1 egg, ½pint of double cream, 1 cup of dry white wine, salt and freshly ground black pepper.

Cook the spaghetti al dente in lightly salted boiling water. Wash it off in a colander for a few minutes in cold water (drain). Put the olive oil in a large frying pan with crushed and finely chopped garlic, let it cook for 1 minute then add the cream and white wine. Let it simmer for 4 minutes, add the salt. Bring to the bubble and add the spaghetti, blend in the egg and freshly ground pepper just before you serve it.

132. Mock Fillets of Sole

2ozs semolina, 2 teaspoonfuls of grated onion, 2 teaspoonfuls of butter, 4 cooked potatoes, ½pint of milk, white sauce, chopped parsley and salt.

Stir the semolina and milk into a saucepan until boiling, add butter and onion, cook slowly for 12 minutes then add mashed potatoes to thicken the mixture. Season with the salt. Turn the mixture out on to a floured board and form into fillet shape pieces. Dip them in egg wash, toss them in breadcrumbs, fry them in deep hot fat and serve with white sauce and parsley.

133. Haricot Bean Patties

½lb haricot beans, 1 onion, 2ozs butter, a pinch of mixed herbs, 1 egg, breadcrumbs, salt and pepper, chopped parsley, 2 tablespoons of grated cheese.

Soak the beans overnight. Then cook with the onion for 1 hour. Put the beans and onion through a sieve and add the butter, cheese, seasoning and eggs to bind. When cool enough, make the mixture into little patties, and egg and breadcrumb them.

Chapter 33
Classification of Foods

Well Balanced Meals

Today one reads and hears so much about diet and its relation to health. Calories and vitamins are now common terms but, nevertheless, too much importance cannot be laid on the part food plays in a heathy life.

One hundred years ago the body still required certain definite elements in food i.e. protein, fats and carbohydrates. No less indispensable were mineral salts which build up bones, nourish nerves and purify the blood and Vitamins A, B, C, D, E, and G.

Classification of Foodstuffs in the 1800's

Foodstuffs were classified either according to their chemical composition or to the work they do to the body.

Proteins are examples of nitrogenous foodstuffs and contain nitrogen and oxygen which are also present in fats and carbohydrates. As already mentioned, protein foods such as meat, fish, milk, eggs and pulses were very easy to get hold of in the eighteenth, never mind nineteenth, century. They are necessary in the diet for repairing worn tissues and for growth. Although physiologists do not all agree with regard to the proportion of protein which is desirable to include in the diet most local authorities today are of the opinion that about 20% of the food consumed in Britain should consist of protein in some form or another.

Fats are valuable as sources of heat and energy. Weight for weight fats yield more than twice as much heat as protein and carbohydrate when 'burnt' in the body.

Carbohydrates are important as they also supply the body with heat and energy. The bulk of our food is made of carbohydrate in some form or other, chiefly starch and sugar. The body obtains its supply of starch from flour and flour based foods, potatoes and cereal foods.

Sugar is taken as cane or beet sugar, honey and also milk and fruit.

Mineral Salts are important in body building as every cell in the body contains them. Calcium salts are especially valuable for the formation of bones and teeth. Fruits and vegetables are both good sources of mineral salts.

Chapter 34
Ices, Confectionery and Desserts

Television has helped the catering trade a great deal with gourmet classes and stories on our great cooks, but before television there were lots of interests in the Victorian homes and one of those interests was Bible Cake. This must be one of the most famous cake recipes and dates back at least to 1830. If a mental picture can be formed of the rather old fashioned and clumsy equipment, perforce used by the Victorian cook, it may be surprising to find that for this recipe the cook needed a Bible — Authorised Version — and, it will be appreciated, a considerable amount of time. So if you have a Bible here is an 1830's recipe:—

134. A Bible Cake
½lb of Judges 6 – 20, 1 tablespoonful of I Samuel 14 – 25, 3 Jeremiah 17 – 11, 2 tablespoons of Judges 4 – 19, ½lb Jeremiah 6 – 20, ½lb Nahum 3 – 12 (chopped), ½lb I Samuel 30 – 12, 2ozs Numbers 17 – 8 (chopped), 1lb I Kings 4 – 22, one teaspoon II Chronicles 9 – 9, pinch of Leviticus 2 – 13, and 1 teaspoonful of Amos 4 – 5.
Mix it all well together and place in a greased baking tin. Bake for 1½ hours Gas 4 350F. Leave it in the tin for 15 minutes before putting it on a wire tray to cool.

135. White Puddings in Skins (1809)
Boil *half a pound of rice in milk till it is soft, having first washed the rice well in warm water. Put it into a sieve to drain, and beat half a pound of Jordan almonds* very fine with *some rose water.* Wash and dry a *pound of currants,* cut in small bits, a *pound of hog's lard,* beat up *six eggs* well, *half a pound of sugar, a large nutmeg, a stick of cinnamon, a little mace and a little salt.* Mix them well together, fill your skins and boil them.

136. Lady Sunderland's Pudding (1811)
Beat up *the yolks of eight eggs with the whites of three,* add to them *five spoonfuls of flour, with half a nutmeg* and put them into *a pint of cream.* Butter the insides of some small basins, fill them half full, and bake them an hour. When done turn them out of the basins and pour over them *melted butter* mixed with *wine and sugar.*

Puddings and cakes have been popular since the first cookery book was written. I wrote a recipe for my good friend Derek Billington when I wrote my first book *The People of Bolton on Cookery* as a thank you for all his help.

137. My Own Bread Pudding
1 pint of milk, ½ pint white breadcrumbs and the same brown breadcrumbs, ¾ oz of butter, 1oz castor sugar, 2 eggs, the grated rind of 1 lemon, apricot jam, 1oz sultanas and a teaspoon of allspice.

Boil the milk, put the breadcrumbs into a basin, add the sugar, butter, sultanas, lemon rind, allspice, mix together and pour on the milk. When it has cooled a little stir in the beaten yolks of egg. Place the mixture in a greased pie dish, and bake for 15 minutes or until set. When it has set and cooled spread on a thick layer of jam, cover with stiffly whisked egg whites, dredge well with castor sugar. Return to the oven, singing *On the road to Mandalay,* after two choruses the meringue should have been browning and ready to serve with a nice white sauce.

OSCAR WILDE was born on 16th October 1854, at 21 Westland Row, Dublin. He was a poet, dramatist, wit and a great lover of fine food. He dressed in the most fashionable clothes of his own style with a green carnation always in his buttonhole. He was resented and scorned by the Marquis of Queensberry who sent Oscar a card at the Albemarle Club, endorsed 'To Oscar Wilde posing as a somdomite' — a mis-spelling which became famous and ultimately led to Oscar being jailed for his beliefs in April 1895 and sent to Reading Goal where he wrote the world famous *Ballad of Reading Goal.* The once editor of *Women's World,* and writer of *Lady Windermere's Fan, The Picture of Dorian Gray* and *The Importance of Being Earnest* was to be convict number C.3.3 for two years. In 1897 he went to live in Paris and died there on the 30th November 1900 at the *Hotel d'Alsace,* Rue des Beaux Arts, Paris. He was buried at Perè-Lachaise, Paris with a tomb of a sphinx over Oscar's resting place. It was England's loss that he was banished because of his personal life. But the man of wit will not be forgotten.

Oscar Wilde *(National Portrait Gallery)*

138. Oscar Wilde Souffle or (The Green Carnation)

1lb green gooseberries (puree), ¼pint of water, 4 tablespoons of granulated sugar, 3 tablespoons of creme de menthe, 4 eggs (separated), 2ozs castor sugar, ¼pint of cream (double), ½oz gelatine, 4 tablespoons water, 3 drops of green colouring, 7 inch diameter souffle dish.

Tie a band of oiled greaseproof paper around the inside of the dish. Beat the egg yolks, puree, sugar in a bowl. Whisk the mixture over heat until it is thick, then remove from the heat and continue whisking until the bowl is cool. Half whip the ¼ pint of cream with the creme de menthe, stir in the gooseberry mixture. Soak the gelatine in water, then dissolve over a gentle heat; add to the souffle with the colouring. When the mixture begins to thicken, whisk egg whites to a firm snow peak, fold in very carefully and turn the souffle into the dish; leave it to set.

139. Blancmange (1811)

There are various methods of making this jelly, but the best, and those most usually practised, are three; the first of which is termed green and is prepared from isinglass in the following manner:

Having dissolved your *isinglass,* put to it *two ounces of sweet* and the same quantity of *bitter almonds,* with some of the *juice of spinach* to make it green, and a *spoonful of French Brandy.* Set it over a stove fire in a saucepan and let it remain till it is almost ready to boil then strain it through a gauze sieve and when it grows thick put it into a melon mould, let it lie till the next day and then turn it out. You may garnish it with red and white flowers.

140. Whipt Syllabub (1811)

Rub a *lump of loaf sugar on the outside of a lemon and put it into a pint of thick cream,* and sweeten it to your taste. Then squeeze in the *juice of a lemon,* and add *a glass of Madeira wine, or French Brandy.* Mill it to a froth with a chocolate mill, take off the froth as it rises and lay it in a hair sieve. Then fill one half of your glasses a little more than half full with white wine and the other half of your glasses a little more than half full with red wine. Then lay on your froth as high as you can but take care that it is well drained in your sieve, otherwise it will mix with the wine, and your syllabub will be spoiled.

Blancmange and syllabubs have not changed that much over the last 200 years. We do not use spinach juice to make them green any more. You can get them ready made or in the powdered form but homemade is far superior.

141. Strawberry Blancmange

1lb of ripe strawberries, 2ozs of gelatine, ¾lb of sugar granulated, juice of a lemon, ½ pint of cream and a pint and half of milk, ¼lb brown sugar.

Pound the strawberries very fine and sprinkle the sugar over them and let them soak for an hour. Press them through a sieve. Dissolve the gelatine in a pint of the milk with a ¼lb of brown sugar, add the rest of the milk and cream when the milk comes to the boil and whisk until warm, then add the strawberries, whisking very quickly together. Add a few drops of lemon juice slowly. Then put into your moulds until set.

142. Whipt Syllabub (Author's recipe)

The nice thing about syllabubs is that it only takes a matter of minutes to make them. *1 pint of whipping cream, 4ozs castor sugar, juice of 1 lemon, 4 tablespoons of brandy, 4 tablespoons of orange curacao, 2 tablespoons of Tia Maria.*

Put the sugar and liquids into a bowl and whisk very fast for 3 minutes, add the whipping cream and whip until stiff. Put the syllabub into champagne glasses and decorate with mint wafers and walnuts. Put into the fridge for an hour before serving.

Ices

Refrigeration machines were very rare in the nineteenth century, the first one being patented as early as 1834. It was a luxury only the rich could afford and not until the 1860s did their popularity come to the British household.

Warnes Model Cookery 1868 on Ices.

> Ice is no longer a luxury confined to the splendid homes of the rich. Sold at the cheap rate of one penny or twopence the pound, it is within reach of the middle classes, and is found of the greatest service to the cook. During the heat of summer when our butter threatens to become oil, a few lumps of ice, placed round and on the pot, will render it good and eatable at a very slight expense.

A gentleman called Ash invented the New "Piston" Freezing Machines at £2. 10 shillings. They were worth their weight in ice. Then came Ash's Filtering Refrigerator.

It is cheaper today to buy our ice cream from the supermarket, but for the sake of history here are some of those wonderful old recipes.

143. Plain Ice Cream

To one pint of cream, add the juice of 1 lemon, half a pound of sugar, a little nutmeg, mix, freeze. If too rich, add a little new milk.

144. Here is one recipe, I tested and do not recommend.

Brown Bread Ice Cream (1860)

Take *a slice of bread, browned in the oven, ½lb sugar, ½pint of milk, 2 sponge biscuits, 1 pint of cream;* put all into a saucepan, stir over a gentle fire, *(like custard), pass through a sieve,* brown 2 slices of bread and make them into breadcrumbs. When the mixture is frozen, add the breadcrumbs with a glass of maraschino.

145. Punch a la Victoria (1870)

The peel of 2 lemons and the juice of 6, the juice of 2 oranges, ½ pint of water, 1 pint of clarified sugar (10ozs), mix, strain, and freeze hard. Add *1 glass of rum, 1 of brandy,* charge the ice again (freeze), as the spirit will bring it down, beat up *the whites of 3 eggs* quite firm, put ¼lb sugar with the whites, *stir it gently in, put it to the ice, and mix slowly (the word freeze hard would mean chill).*

146. Vanilla Ice Cream

The modern method is sure to be the better method than Ash's old fashioned crank freezer (ice and salt method). The most common freezer was a metal container placed within a wooden bucket. The space between the two was packed with rock salt and crushed ice (about 3 parts ice to 1 part salt).

Here's the more up to date method.

1 pint of milk, 8ozs castor sugar, 2 eggs, ¾ pint of cream, ½ teaspoon of vanilla.

Stir together the milk, castor sugar and well beaten eggs. Heat in a double saucepan till they thicken. Allow to cool, then add the cream, beat well and put to freeze in the freezer, or ice tray of a refrigerator.

147. Charlotte Russe Marie-Antoine Careme

Line the bottom of a mould with *sponge fingers* cut in heart shape and fingers all the way round the side of the mould, they should be protruding about ¾ inch above the mould.

Blend *18ozs sugar, 16 egg yolks* in a small saucepan over a low heat. When the mixture is smooth moisten with *1¾ pints of milk,* which has boiled. Flavour this with *vanilla,* add *1oz of gelatine* dissolved in cold water, keep stirring until mixture thickens, transfer this into a clean cold bowl to cool, stir occasionally, as soon as the mixture begins to set, fold in *1 pint of cream with 2ozs sugar (whipped), fold into the russe mould and set.*

148. Sally Lunns Eliza Acton 1856 (adapted by the Author)
Into a basin put *¾lb of flour and with it mix ¼ pint of brewer's yeast,* and *½ pint of milk* which has been warmed. Cover the basin and let it stand in a warm place for 2 hours. Meanwhile, rub *2ozs butter into another 4ozs of flour,* add this to the sponge in the basin and then beat in *2 eggs,* one at a time. Let it stand again for ½ an hour, then knead the dough well. Use it for half-filling a round tin, let it stand in a warm place until the dough reaches to the top of the tin, and then bake it in a quick oven. *Castor sugar,* moistened with *milk,* is the best glaze to brush over the top.

149 Cossack's Plum Pudding Alexis Soyer (1855)
Put into a basin *1lb of flour, ¾lb of raisins* (stoned if time be allowed), *¾lb of the fat of salt pork* (well washed, cut into small squares, or chopped), *2 tablespoons of sugar or treacle; and ½ pint of water;* mix all together, put into a cloth tied lightly, boil for 4 hours, and serve. If time will not admit, boil only two hours, though four are preferable. How to spoil the above and wound it. Add anything to it.

Confectionery was very popular in Victorian England. Here I have revised some of those recipes for you to try.

150. Barley Sugar 1887
1lb of castor sugar, ½ pint of water, white of 1 egg and vanilla essence.
Put the sugar and water into a pan. When dissolved put over a moderate heat, and when it is just beginning to warm add beaten white of egg. Stir well, and when boiling remove scum, and boil until perfectly clear. Strain through a muslin, and boil up again when done, a little dropped into cold water should be very brittle and snap easily. A flat slab or marbleslab is better than a dish when doing sweets. Pour on the slab and cut into strips. Dip the hand in cold water and roll and twist the sticks, and when cold, you may dust a little sifted sugar over.

151. Chocolate Walnuts 1892

½oz gelatine, 10ozs icing sugar, ½ pint of cold water, 1oz glucose powder, a few drops of vanilla essence, some split halves of walnuts, 2ozs melted chocolate.

Put the gelatine and ½ of the sugar with the water into a saucepan and stir over the cooker (moderate) until boiling. Add the glucose and stir until dissolved. Put the remainder of the icing sugar on a slab and melt the chocolate in a saucepan. Put the hot sugar mixture into the centre of the dry sugar, add to it the melted chocolate and the vanilla essence and work all to a smooth paste. Make the mixture up into small balls; on each side of these press the halves of the walnuts and put in a cool place to harden.

152. Turkish Delight 1889

1oz Gelatine, ¾ teaspoonful tartaric Acid, 2 teacups of castor sugar, ½ teacup of cold water, ¾ cupful of boiling water, 1 teaspoonful of vanilla essence, juice of 1 lemon, and a little cochineal to colour.

Soak gelatine in cold water for 2 hours. Put the sugar into the boiling water. Boil for 7 minutes with tartaric acid. Add lemon and pour over the gelatine. Stir well; add essence and colouring. Pour into prepared plates.

153. Mother Eve's Pudding from *Enquire Within* 1891

If you want a good pudding, to teach you I'm willing,
Take two pennyworth of eggs, when twelve for a shilling,
And of the same fruit that Eve had once chosen,
Well pared and well chopped, at least half a dozen,
Six ounces of bread (let your maid eat the crust),
The crumbs must be grated as small as the dust,
Six ounces of currants from the stones you must sort,
Lest they break out your teeth, and spoil all your sport,
Six ounces of sugar won't make it too sweet,
Some salt and some nutmeg will make it complete,
Three hours let it boil, without hurry or flutter,
And then serve it up, without sugar or butter.

Basically known as rhyme pudding in the early nineteenth century, it sounds like a Kitchener recipe to me.

154. A queer Kind of Cake about 1842

A fashionable young lady visited a cooking school, where her attention was equally divided between a new dress worn by an acquaintance and directions for making a cake.

Upon returning home she undertook to write down the recipe. Take *2lbs of flour,* 3 rows of plaiting down the front, *the whites of 2 eggs* cut bias, *a pint of milk* ruffled around the neck, *½lb currants* with 7 yards of bead trimming, *grated lemon peel* with Spanish lace fichu. Stir well and add a semi-fitting paletot with visite sleeves. Butter the pan with Brazilian topaz necklace, and garnish with icing and jet passementerie. Bake in a moderately hot oven until the over skirt is tucked from waist down on either side, and finish with large satin bow.

Author's note:— This is one cake that does not need dressing up!

Chapter 35
How the Cook would Pick her Produce

Skill was required in purchasing food. Pork was a dangerous food to buy in the markets because if you were not experienced in buying you would have a bad case of food poisoning. The experienced cook would only buy from a respectable butcher. The fat of pork should be firm, lean and white, finely grained with the rind, thin and smooth. If the flesh was clammy or very sticky to the touch they would know the pork was high. They would tell if bacon was fresh by the colour. If it was yellow they would not buy it. Hams were tried by sticking a skewer up to the knuckle. If when it was drawn out it had a nice smell the ham was good. A bad smell would be perceived if it was tainted.

Turkey,— the cock bird, when young, has a smooth black leg with a short spur. The eyes are bright and full, and the feet supple when fresh; the absence of these signs denotes age and staleness. The hen was judged by the same rules.

Geese,— in young geese the feet and bills will be yellow and free from hair when fresh. The feet should be pliable. If they are stiff then the geese is stale. These methods still apply today.

How did they know if the butter was good, the cheese maggoty or the eggs bad. In that order from *The Young Woman's Companion* 1811 here are some very different methods of detection.

Butter

The greatest care is necessary in buying this article to avoid being deceived. You must not trust to the taste the sellers give you as they will frequently give you a taste of one lump, and sell you another. On choosing salt butter, trust rather to your smell than taste by putting a knife into it, and applying it to your nose. If the butter is in a cask have it unhooped and thrust in your knife between the staves, into the middle of it, for by the artful mode of package, and the ingenuity of those who send it from the country, the butter on the top of the cask is often much better than the middle.

Buying eggs *(Hannah Firmin)*

Cheese

Before you purchase this article take particular notice of the coat or rind. If the cheese is old with a rough and ragged coat or dry top, you may expect to find little worms or mites in it. If it is moist, spongy or full of holes there will be reason to suspect it is maggoty.

Whenever you perceive any perished places on the outside, be sure to probe the bottom of them, for though the hole in the coat may be small, the perished part within may be considerable.

Eggs

To judge properly of an egg, put the greater end to your tongue, and if it feels warm it is new, but if cold, it is stale, and according to the degree of heat or cold there is in the egg you will judge of its staleness or newness.

Another method is hold it up against the sun or a candle and if the yolk appears round and the white clear and fair it is a mark of goodness, but if the yolk if broken, and the white cloudy or muddy, the egg is a bad one.

Some people in order to try the goodness of an egg, put it into a pan of cold water. In this case the fresher the egg is the sooner it will sink to the bottom, but if it is addled or rotten, it will swim on the surface of the water.

The best method of preserving eggs, is to keep them in meal or bran, though some place them in wood-ashes, with their small ends downwards. When necessity obliges you to keep them for any length of time bury them in salt. It preserves in any climate.

Chapter 36
Butter and Cheese

Compound Butters

Beckman, in his *History of Inventions*, states that butter was not used either by the Greeks or Romans in cooking, nor was it brought upon their tables at certain meals, as it is the custom today.

In England it has been made from time immemorial, though the art of making compound butters only really started at the beginning of the 19th century. It is mentioned in *The Woman's Companion* of 1806: "If you feed your cow parsnips you will get a dark yellowish butter, if you feed them turnip the butter will be stronger and white, adding spinach darkens the butter even more." If we did this method today I am sure this would work but the later Victorian methods were far better.

Since many of these flavoured butters may be used as spreads as well as fillings, it may be as well to mention these first.

These consist of best quality butter mixed with various ingredients which impart flavour and often colour. You should not make them up until they are required, for they will undergo change in colour and slight fermentation due to the fact that they are mixtures.

For decoration they are piped through a savoy bag fitted with a star nozzle. All butter should be tasted during preparation for seasoning as well as the mixture consistency.

Coloured Butters

These butters are mixtures coloured by flavouring the ingredient incorporated in them.

Yellow	Egg butter, the depth of colour depends on the amount of hard boiled egg yolk used.
Black	Truffle butter
White	Salted butter
Cream	Lightly worked salted butter
Red	Lobster butter
Green	Herb butter
Pink	Crayfish, ham, cayenne or tomato butter
Pale Green	Lauris or Spinach butter
Grey	Caviar butter

155. Compound Butter

For all the recipes for compound butters I am about to show you, use 4ozs, unless stated. The ingredients are pounded or blended to a puree and mixed with the butter which is then passed through a fine wire sieve, and wrapped in a cold damp cloth and put to one side for an hour (to ½lb of butter).

Almond Butter	2ozs blanched almonds
Anchovy Butter	2ozs drained anchovy fillets
Asparagus Butter	4ozs cooked green asparagus tips
Black Grape Butter	Black grapes peeled and pipped
Caviar Butter	2ozs Caviar
Cayenne Butter	¼ teaspoon of cayenne
Chervil Butter	2ozs chervil blanched and refreshed
Chestnut Butter	2ozs chestnut puree
Cherry Butter	2ozs cherries stoned and peeled
Chocolate Butter	2ozs cocoa
Curry Butter	1oz onion and 1oz curry powder
Damson Butter	Damsons peeled and stoned
Egg Butter	2ozs hard boiled egg yolks
Garlic Butter	2ozs garlic, boiled for 4 minutes
Gruyere Butter	2ozs grated gruyere cheese
Ginger butter	2ozs ground ginger
Ham Butter	4ozs lean finely chopped ham, 2ozs chopped onion.
Herb Butter	2ozs mixed herbs (fine herbs)
Hazelnut Butter	2ozs roasted hazelnuts
Lobster Butter	4ozs of cooked lobster

All the above can be used on bread, toast, biscuits or vol-au-vents.

Cheeses

The oldest British cheese is Cheshire, savoury and mellow, yet the most popular I would say is English Cheddar, strong yellow with a close creamy texture. The best cheese for cooking because it has a high fat content is Lancashire with its crumbly texture and off white colour. To me the King of cheeses is Stilton; with a glass of old vintage port there is no better way to round off a meal.

The English have been making cheeses for hundreds of years. It was well known over 3,000 years ago in the Bible — 1st book of Samuel, chapter 17, verses 17 and 18.

> And Jesse said unto David his son, Take now for thy brethren an ephah of this parched corn, and these ten loaves, and run to the camp to thy brethren; And carry these ten cheeses unto the captain of their thousand . . .

It takes one gallon of full cream milk to make one pound of cheese, as a concentrated form of milk consists of ⅓ water, ⅓ fat and ⅓ protein with Vitamins A, D, B, calcium and iron.

The 19th century ways of making cheese are still being used on the old farms off the beaten tracks of the old villages of England. They would put the milk into a large tub, warming part of it to a degree of finger warmth, if it got too hot the cheese would be tough. Put in as much rennet as would turn (rennet being the stomach of a calf). Then they would let it stand until completely turned. Then they would cut the curd down with a skimming dish and let it stand until completely turned. Then they would cut the curd down with a skimming dish and let it separate. Then they would gather it with their hands very gently towards the side of the tub, letting the whey (milk substance) pass through the fingers till it is cleared, it is ladled off as it collects.

156. Stilton Sauce
The cost of making cheese today is very expensive if you are only making small quantities. A fellow chef of mine had a very good recipe for *the crust of Stilton.* He would ground it down very fine, add it to a *basic roux,* with *a tot of brandy, ground black pepper, touch of garlic salt, cream and paprika* and then he would pour this beautiful sauce over a rare Entrecote Steak. Thank you John Sherry!

Chapter 37
"The Caterer and Hotelkeeper"

The Caterer and Hotelkeeper magazine which published *The Caterer and Refreshment Contracters' Gazette* in London on April 6th 1878, price 7d, have very kindly given me permission to use the very first issue of their then monthly Journal.

The *Caterer* of today is the top magazine for the hotel proprietor, chef and caterer. This was so even at its launch in April 1878 when John Plummer edited the magazine. His principal object was to furnish business information and form a trade encyclopedia for the caterer and in this respect the magazine has remained unchanged.

Here is a quotation from that first *Caterer:*

> In placing the first issue of *The Caterer* before those to whose interests it directly appeals, he entertains not the slightest doubt that the earnest and independent spirit by which its columns are animated will become duly recognised and secure for it their hearty co-operation and active support. A fair field and no favour is all that is asked. This granted, no exertion will be spared to make *The Caterer* one of the most successful and useful trade journals of the present day.

The format of the magazine has obviously changed with the times and it now includes menus, a letter page, property sales and worldwide job vacancies which amongst many other things have gone to produce a useful trade journal for the present day.

The original magazine had within its cover many things which remain today such as food prices and the advertising of equipment but thankfully the list of court cases involving household staff and their punishments has gone by the board.

A recent step forward for the publishers of *The Caterer and Hotelkeeper* is the forthcoming launch of a new magazine *The Chef* which will be published on a quarterly basis and will be devoted entirely to the chef, including articles on up and coming chefs and commercial enterprises.

You can see from the photograph of the old and new *Caterer* the difference in style and presentation.

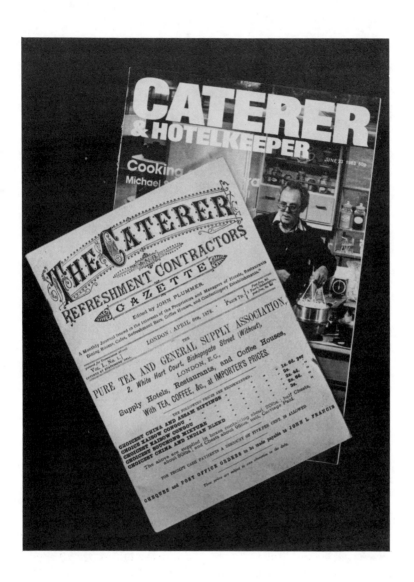

The cover of the First Edition of *The Caterer* with a modern
cover superimposed *(by permission of the Caterer and
Hotelkeeper).*

LEGAL AND MAGISTERIAL NOTES.

The Right of Light.—In the Queen's Bench Division of the High Court of Justice, the late case of Hall *v.* Moore raised a curious question as to the rights of persons possessed of houses to the usual and accustomed light coming to their windows. The question was whether the right is to be limited in this way—that it is a right only to the light sufficient for the purpose of the particular occupation, or whether it is an absolute right to the usual and accustomed degree of light coming to the premises. It had arisen thus:—The plaintiff sued for obstruction of the old lights of his house in Wapping, and there was no doubt it was proved, at the trial before the Lord Chief Justice, that the obstruction had diminished the degree or quantity of light formerly coming into the house. But then it was urged that the house was used as a cook-shop and coffee-house, and that the degree of light left was good enough for the purpose; so that the damages should be nominal. The Lord Chief Justice did not take that view, and left it to the jury to say, in all the circumstances of the case, what was the damage which had been sustained, and on that direction the jury gave substantial damages. This was an application to set aside that verdict on the ground of misdirection. After a long argument, it appeared that though there were authorities both ways, yet that the preponderance of authority was very greatly in favour of the view that the right to the light was absolute; and on that view the Court ultimately affirmed the direction of the Lord Chief Justice and upheld the judgment for the plaintiff. This is a most important decision, inasmuch as it authoritatively lays down the principle that the usual and accustomed light of a place of public refreshment may not be interfered with, save with the consent of the owner. There is nothing new in this principle, but the decision is the first, we believe, recorded in favour of a dining establishment.

Refreshment-House Licenses.—At the Westminster Police Court, Mr. Thomas Bates, of 141, King's Road, Chelsea, was summoned for keeping a refreshment-house without a license.—The house in question is a ham-and-beef shop. On the morning of the 18th of March an excise officer and others were served with ham sandwiches, which they ate in front of the counter.—Defendant did not deny the fact. He had several such shops in London, and if the people liked to eat their sandwiches in the shop they did so, or they could take them home. The real business was selling ham, beef, etc., to be taken away and consumed. If he had infringed the law he had done so unwittingly.—Mr. Woolrych said the decisions of the superior court were against the defendant. He fined the defendant £3, one-fourth of the penalty, and recommended the commissioners of excise to reduce that sum to £2 2s.—Mr. Jacob Beadle, of 369, King's Road, Chelsea, coffee-house keeper, was convicted of selling coffee without a license, at a quarter past eleven on the night of the 18th instant, and was find a similar amount with a similar recommendation.—Mr. George Bolton, of Leete Street, and Manor Street, Chelsea, was summoned for selling fried fish without a license, but the matter was compromised and withdrawn. We shall next have the bakers summoned for allowing their customers to eat the penny loaves purchased by them before leaving the shop. Such prosecutions are ridiculous. Several cases of a somewhat similar character are reported from Middleton, in Lancashire, where a number of persons who sell "tripe," and add to that offence the further enormity of allowing it to be "consumed on the premises," were summoned by the excise for having neglected to take out licenses as keepers of "refreshment-houses." The lowest penalty that the magistrate could impose was £5. This was inflicted in one case, and the Bench, remarking that "the law was very hard," recommended the authorities to mitigate the penalty still further. Such a recommendation shows pretty clearly what is the opinion entertained by our magisterial authorities respecting what is virtually a tax on the sale of food.

Robberies by Restaurant Servants.—At the Mansion House recently, Susan Fenderson and Ellen Lees were charged with larceny. The prisoners were kitchenmaids in the service of Messrs. Mabey and Sons, restaurant keepers, Gresham House, and were stopped by the police, who noticed their bulky appearance. They denied having anything about them belonging to their masters, but on being searched at the police-station a bag of considerable size was found under each of their dresses. That carried by Fenderson contained two pounds of cooked meat, and some carrots, turnips, and potatoes; and that by Lees held three pounds of meat, some butter, and vegetables. This they admitted was the property of Messrs. Mabey. Alderman Sir A. Lusk, M.P., sentenced them each to seven days' hard labour.

Waitresses and their Employers.—In the case of Jewell *v.* Bird, heard a few days ago in the Shoreditch County Court, the defendant, who is the proprietor of a café restaurant near Oxford Street, advertised for two waitresses. The advertisement was answered by the plaintiffs, who are two sisters, the result being that both were engaged by defendant at a salary of £12 a year, with a month's notice. According to one of the plaintiffs, she was asked by defendant to serve a customer with a cup of coffee, but owing to some noise in the street did not hear what was said. Her sister, who was nearer defendant, seeing that she had not heard the order, told her of it, and the customer was then served. Defendant shortly after addressed the plaintiffs, saying he would be glad if they left, and ended by telling them to get out. No reason was given for the dismissal, and the plaintiffs now sued for a month's wages each. For the defence, it was shown that the plaintiffs were several times remonstrated with by the defendant for paying too much attention to some of the customers, and neglecting others. As plaintiffs had promised to improve, but did not, defendant felt bound to tell them they might go. He, however, denied dismissing them. The Judge said it appeared to him that the young girls did not do anything that was absolutely wrong, and he believed their character was irreproachable. At the same time, he thought there was some ground for defendant's complaints, and as he did not think the plaintiffs had shown a disposition to please the defendant, the dismissal, if it took place, was, under the circumstances, justifiable. For this reason the plaintiffs were only entitled to a week's wages, for which he accordingly gave judgment.

A Curious Dispute.—In the Clerkenwell County Court Mr. Wm. Henry Collier, of Southend, Essex, refreshment-house keeper, brought an action against Mr. John Gonzius, of 52, Pentonville Road, confectioner, for the recovery of certain goods of the value of £34 11s. 6d., and for damages caused by detention of said goods, £11s.; total, £35 12s. 6d.—Plaintiff stated that he disposed of the refreshment-house, 52, Pentonville Road, to the defendant on the 29th of September last, and asked defendant to be allowed to leave some things stowed in the cellar for a few weeks, to which the defendant assented; but when he went for the things defendant would not let him have them unless he paid 6s. for a gate, which he alleged plaintiff had broken, but he had not broken it. On cross-examination he said he went for the goods at the end of a month or six weeks. Defendant put in a counter claim for use and occupation of the cellar in which the goods were stowed, and stated that plaintiff asked him to be allowed to leave the goods for a couple of weeks, and he would pay defendant for the use of the cellar and cupboard so long as the things were in them, but no sum was mentioned. Plaintiff had the key of the cellar, and he did not know what was in it.—The Judge said he could not see that any agreement was made for the payment of rent. He therefore gave judgment for plaintiff for the amount claimed, but if the goods were given up to plaintiff, damages 1s. only and costs; the counter claim being disallowed.

Buying Oysters.—In the City of London Court, the case of Teppler *v.* Barber has furnished a hint to buyers of oysters. It was a claim for compensation for three barrels of oysters bought by the plaintiff, at 16s. 8d. per barrel. When taken home they were found to be unfit to be eaten. He bought four barrels, the top of one of which only was open, and he was debarred from seeing what kind of oysters he was purchasing. This was denied by the representative of the defendant, who said that it was by the choice of the plaintiff himself these barrels were assigned to him. No one prevented him examining the oysters. Ultimately a verdict was given for the defendant.

Bankruptcy Cases.—In the London Bankruptcy Court, Percival Reed, described as of the London Restaurant, 191, Fleet Street, and of Chancery Lane, restaurateur and wine merchant, has presented a petition for liquidation, his debts amounting to about £30,000, and assets, comprising plant, machinery,

Legal Notes from *The Caterer*, 1878.

154

and furniture, and also stock of the value of £1000. Upon the application of Mr. Doria, Mr. Registrar Spring-Rice appointed Mr. C. L. Nichols, accountant, Queen Victoria Street, as receiver and manager of th state, the nomination being supported by creditors for £55w.——Richard Goundry, Upper Thames Street, trading as Goundr¯ and Company, has petitioned for the liquidation of his affairs, estimating his liabilities at £23,300, and assets £7853. Mr. Lucas applied for the appointment of Mr. Izard, accountant, Eastcheap, as receiver and manager of the estate, and for an interim order restraining two actions. The application was supported by creditors, and Mr. Registrar Hazlitt made the appointment, and granted an interim injunction.

Alleged Fraudulent Bill of Sale.—In the Bankruptcy Court, in the matter of John Kemp, a refreshment house keeper of Paddington. Mr. Registrar Hazlitt has given judgment upon a motion by Mr. E. C. Chatterley, the trustee of the estate, to declare null and void a certain bill of sale given over the whole of the debtor's estate to secure an alleged advance of £300 by a Mr. George Box, of Campden Road, Islington. The bill of sale was impeached on the ground of fraud and collusion. The arguments had been heard on a previous day, Mr. De Gex, Q.C., and Mr. Brennan appearing for the trustee, and Mr. E. Cooper Willis for the bill of sale holder. The learned Registrar, in giving judgment, was of opinion that the bill of sale was fraudulent and collusive, and ordered the proceeds of the sale of the estate in question, which had been paid into court, to be handed over to the trustee, the bill of sale holder to pay the costs of the application.

Conditions of Public-House Extension.—At the recent Finsbury Licensing Meeting, Mr. John Farren, proprietor of the Thatched House, Essex Road, applied to be allowed to extend his premises, and submitted his plans.—The surveyor said that the premises would be much enlarged, but there was no accommodation for workmen to cook their dinners. The tap-room would be confined entirely to that purpose.—Sir James Tyler, the chairman of the Licensing Board, said he would oppose the granting of the extension on that very ground. It seemed as if the enlargement was only intended to give more room for drinking.—Mr. Alderman Figgins said it was of the utmost importance that in all cases there should be ample accommodation for the working classes to cook their food. It was a stipulation that ought to be insisted on in every case. The Chairman said the case would be deferred, to enable the bench to visit the house and view it for themselves.

A Reason for Refusing License.—At the annual licensing meeting of the Finsbury Division, Thomas Gregory, 26, High Street, Islington, oyster and fish shop-keeper, applied for a beer license. The applicant stated that he intended to supply his customers only with beer, and to retail it over the counter. He did not open on Sundays, and would be satisfied with a six days' license. The Bench thought that as the applicant had done a good business for so many years he would not suffer much from the want of a license. They therefore refused the license.

MARKETS AND MARKETING.

In our next number we shall commence a series of monthly Market Reports and Marketing Notes.

TO CORRESPONDENTS.

The Second Number of the "CATERER" will appear May 4, 1878.

All communications of a Literary nature, Books for Review, &c., should be addressed to Mr. John Plummer; and all Business communications to the Publishers, J. Gilbert Smith & Co. Editorial and Publishing Offices—67, Leadenhall Street, London, E.C.

The Caterer,

AND

Refreshment Contractor's Gazette

WILL BE PUBLISHED

On the FIRST SATURDAY of EACH MONTH.

Price SEVENPENCE; or, by Post, EIGHTPENCE.

Annual Subscription, Post Free, 6s. 6d.

SCALE OF CHARGES FOR ADVERTISEMENTS.

One Page	...	...	£5 0 0
Half ditto	...	...	2 15
One-third ditto	...	...	2 0 0
Quarter Page	...	...	1 12 0
One-eighth ditto	...	...	0 18 0
One-sixteenth ditto	...	...	0 10 0

Special Rates for Wrapper and Pages preceding and following literary matter.

The above Scale of Charges will be subject to a LIBERAL REDUCTION for Advertisements extending over a period of time, if ordered in advance.

Accounts payable Quarterly, at the end of March, June, September and December.

Advertisements of Businesses Wanted, or for Disposal, Employers wanting assistants, Partnerships. Sundry Articles for sale or Exchange, are charged at the rate of 3s. 6d. for five lines and under ; every additional line, 6d., payable in advance.

Advertisements of Assistants, Waiters, and other employés wanting situations, 1s. 6d. for four lines ; every additional line, 4d., payable in advance.

Orders for Advertisements and Remittances should be forwarded to

J. GILBERT SMITH & CO.,

Offices of "The Caterer,"

67, LEADENHALL STREET, LONDON, E.C

Legal Notes (continued).

PARISIAN WAITERS.

There is a great difference between English and Parisian waiters, a result in some measure of the difference in the dining characteristics of the two countries. The Englishman is always in a hurry to get through his meal; the Frenchman, on the contrary, regards it as an affair which does not admit of haste. If he cannot give the requisite time to his dinner, he would rather forego it altogether. Hence while the English waiter is compelled to be continually on the move, and to rapidly jerk out his replies in most laconic fashion, his Parisian brother has sufficient leisure to practise the many little niceties which impart such a charm to a meal in one of the numerous elegant and tastefully furnished restaurants which stud the leading thoroughfares of the French capital. He is always polite, obliging, and attentive; virtues which are found efficacious in extracting sous and occasional half-francs from the pockets of his employer's customers. Of course there are exceptions to the rule, for we have met with garçons who not only insisted in setting down to us articles we had never seen or tasted, but actually attempted to bully us into the payment of fees higher than those ordinarily given. Attendants of this class, however, inflict such serious injury on the interest of their employers that their services are readily dispensed with. In many of the Parisian establishments the waiters have no remuneration save the fees given by the customers and their meals. In others they receive certain fixed wages, to which the fees are regarded as supplementary. On the whole, however, they obtain less than is received by the waiters at an ordinary English hotel. They are, however, expected to keep themselves clean and decently dressed, and how they effect this is sometimes not a little perplexing to the uninitiated. A Parisian waiter without a clean apron or napkin is a rare sight in a respectable café or restaurant. We once saw a garçon who was evidently very uncomfortable. He walked about in a most depressed condition, and we could not help imagining that he was suffering from some serious misfortune. Presently we beheld him gazing stealthily at the napkin under his arm. It certainly possessed no pretensions to snowy whiteness, having apparently been in use a couple of days. After a time he disappeared for a few moments. When he returned his features were radiant with smiles, and in his hands was a fresh, clean napkin. This love of cleanliness often becomes a kind of second nature, and an experienced waiter would no more dare to appear with an untidy shirt-front or a soiled apron, than in the sooty attire of a charcoal dealer.

The use of the jacket in place of the tail-coat is almost universal, and this, combined with the large white aprons worn, aids very materially in decreasing the cost of clothing, besides tending to prevent or conceal that shiny appearance which too frequently reveals the venerable age of an English waiter's attire. The waiter rarely assists in culinary operations. His duties commence with the opening of the premises in the morning, generally about six o'clock. He sweeps the floor, dusts the chairs and tables, placing several of the latter on the pavement in front of the windows; sees that the water-bottles, cruets, lucifer-stands, and other articles are properly replenished; and otherwise prepares for the coming business of the day. He then retires, to re-appear after a short interval as clean and spruce as if he had just stepped out of a milliner's band-box. For at least two or three hours there is little business, and by way of beguiling the time, François amuses himself with a game at dominoes or a perusal of one of the morning papers, for the French are great newspaper readers, even the apple-seller at the corner of the rue being unhappy until she has obtained a peep at Le Petit Journal, a small half-penny daily, about half the size of the Echo, which is said to have a circulation of half a million copies daily. François is too poor to afford the pleasures of married life, but he is extremely economical, and if he is fortunate enough to escape the conscription, he often saves sufficient to enable him to become a restaurant-keeper on his own account. When he marries, it is generally some pretty grisette whose acquaintance he has made during one of his holiday excursions to the barrières, at the cheap bals in the neighbourhood of which his habitual politeness and natural gaiety cause his presence to become regarded with pleasure.

Of a very different type indeed is the head waiter at one of the grand hotels in which everything is ruled to splendour. The aristocratic air with which he replies to the queries of customers who have not engaged the principal apartments, or with whom economy is an object, is very edifying. He is frequently mistaken by unsophisticated Britons for a nobleman in reduced circumstances. Yet he is at bottom a thoroughly unpretentious and good-natured fellow, the stiffness of demeanour and impressive attitudes which form his characteristics during business time being, in fact, a clever bit of acting. He has to attend on customers with whom what may be termed the artificialities of life have become familiar, and is compelled to conduct himself accordingly. A French writer, noticing this fact, states that it is not difficult to ascertain the general character of the customers of any given hotel by simply studying that of the attendants. In several of the larger Parisian hotels the guests are terribly fastidious, finding fault with the least trifle, and making Jules, despite his stately presence, extremely nervous lest he should be called to account by his employer. His dignity is, indeed, dearly purchased, and when his savings are sufficient to enable him to start in business on his own account, after marrying Mademoiselle Henrietta, from the milliner's shop on the adjoining boulevard, he gladly abdicates the uncongenial position which he has so long occupied to his great discomfort, and, it must be confessed, pecuniary advantage.

Preserved Horse-Radish.—In America many grocers and other dealers have for sale grated horse-radish, which they claim will keep a whole year, if left unopened. It is done up in wide-mouthed bottles, tightly corked and sealed over. It is believed to be preserved by means of what is termed Appert's process, which is as follows : The juice or semiliquid article to be preserved is introduced into strong bottles, sufficient space being left for the expansion of the liquid. The bottles being well corked, and the corks secured with stout cord, is placed in a vessel of sufficient depth. A cloth or a thin board with holes is laid under the bottles, and straw is packed between them to prevent breakage. The vessel is then filled with cold water to a height sufficient to cover the bottles up to the shoulder, placed over a gentle fire, and the water slowly brought to ebullition. The boiling is kept up for about ten minutes, when the vessel may be removed from the fire, and the whole allowed to cool down. Lastly, the bottles are sealed by dipping the top in melted sealing-wax. Something like this is practised by our manufacturers of preserved fruits, but we do not believe it has hitherto been used, so far as this country is concerned, for preserving horse-radish.

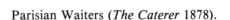

Parisian Waiters (*The Caterer* 1878).

NOTICE.

THIS PAGE

HAS BEEN TAKEN BY A FIRM OF

WHOLESALE POTATO MERCHANTS,

BUT OWING TO CHANGES IN THEIR STYLE
AND OTHER ARRANGEMENTS NOW PENDING,

THEY PREFER RESERVING

ALL PARTICULARS

For the Next and Subsequent Issues.

An Unusual Advertisement (*The Caterer* 1878).

Chapter 38
Wines, Ales and Beverages

One of the first recorded events in history is that Noah when he left the Ark planted a vineyard. Noah knew how to multiply and vineyards all over the world have been doing so ever since. The opening of the 19th century saw wines from the Cape and Constantia. Not until 1854 did we also see wines from Australia come into the English market. Hock was very fashionable with soda water and Burgundy was more popular than a glass of claret; Hermitage was one of the good wines of Portugal and Spain. Wines from Italy and Germany came a little later but were well worth waiting for.

Learning and appreciating wine is not easy. The years of experience that go into learning have fruitful compensations and really you have to be gifted to be a walking book on wines.

What Wine to Dine with
Hors d'Oeuvre, Oysters or Caviar; Hocks, Pouilly, Chablis or Vouvray
Soup; Dry Sherry
Fish; Moselle, Barsac or Graves.
Entrees; Burgundy, Chianti or Claret (I recommend a claret).
Roast; Red Burgundy or Chateau-bottled claret.
Game; Claret, Burgundy or Rhône Hermitage.
Dessert; Champagne or Sauternes (Champagne can really be served at any course).
Cheese; Rich sherry, Burgundy, Rhône or Old Port, Hermitage.
Coffee; Old Brandies or Liqueurs.

Ice should never be placed in wine.
Wine glasses should always be polished before use.
Never use the same glass for two different wines.
Champagne should be served at 42f.
Dry wines are served before sweet wines.
White wines are served before red wines.
Young wines are served before old wines.
Never serve vintage red wines with shellfish and fish.
Never serve vintage sweet white wines with game.

Brillat-Savarin: "The correct order of service of wines is to begin with the most temperate and progress to the headiest and most fragrant."

There are no rigid rules on wine, it really is your own personal taste, the above is just a guide to help you.

Homemade wines are still as popular today as they were 150 years ago. Here are a few recipes from *Warnes Model Cookery* 1868.

157. Blackberry Wine

1lb of sugar to 2lb of blackberry juice, a ¼ pint of gin or brandy.

Cover a quantity of blackberries with water, and put them into an oven (moderate) to draw the juice out of them. Strain them through a sieve and leave them to ferment for 15 days.

Afterwards add a 1lb of sugar to 2 quarts of juice with a ¼ pint of gin or brandy. When bottled, do not cork it too close.

158. Mock Champagne (1868)

To every quart of grapes add a quart of water; to every gallon of juice, allow 3lb of loaf sugar, and ½oz of gelatine to every 10 gallons of wine; and a quart of brandy to every 5 gallons.

Pick the grapes when full-grown and just beginning to change colour, bruise them in a tub, pour in the water and let them stand for 3 days, stirring once each day. Then press the fruit through a muslin, let it stand for 4 hours, pour it carefully from any sediment and add to it the sugar. Barrel it, (bottle it) and put the bung slightly in.

At the end of 3 weeks put in the gelatine, (previously dissolved in some of the liquor). Stir it again for 3 days once a day, and at the last stirring add the brandy. In 4 days bung it down close, and in six months it should be bottled and the corks tied down and wired.

159. To Make George IV Milk Punch (1868)

2 quarts of rum, peel of 12 lemons, peel of 2 seville oranges, 2 quarts of cold spring water, 1lb of loaf sugar, 1 pint of lemon juice, 1 nutmeg, 1 pint of strong green tea, a ¼ pint of maraschino and Madeira, 1 pint of boiling milk.

Mix all together, and then stir in the new milk boiling hot. Let it stand for 6 hours, then pour it through a jelly bag or muslin until it is perfectly clear, then bottle it off for use.

If you quarter the ingredients this is a lovely punch to serve at Birthday parties.

160. Cup—From the "Blues" (1868)

4 quarts of water, 2 bottles of cider, 1 bottle of perry, 1 pint of sherry, 2 large glasses of brandy, 2 of rum, 2 bottles of Champagne will improve this punch also.

161. Superior Claret Cup

2 bottles of claret, 1 of champagne, 3 glasses of sherry, 1 of noyau, ½ lb of ice, 1 sprig of borage, or a few slices of cucumber, sugar if required. Mix, put all the above ingredients into a silver cup, pass a napkin through one of the handles, that the edge of the cup may be wiped after the contents have been partaken of and hand it round to each person.

162. Sherry Cobbler

½ pint of sherry, a little mint, a teaspoonful of sugar, a large quantity of crushed ice, 2 slices of lemon and a bottle of soda water all mixed together.

163. Porter Cup

1 quart of porter, ½ pint of sherry, 4 slices of lemon and a little nutmeg all well mixed with *crushed ice.*

164. Stag's Heart Water (1836)

Take *four handfuls of balm and a handful of sweet marjoram; rosemary flowers clove-gill flowers dried, rosebuds dried and borage flowers, of each an ounce, marigold flowers half an ounce, lemon peel two ounces, mace and cardamum thirty grains of each; cinnamon sixty grains; yellow and white sanders, of each a quarter of an ounce; shavings of hartshorn an ounce and the peels of nine oranges.* Cut them very small and pour upon them *two quarts of the best white wine.* Stop it very close and let it infuse nine or ten days in a cellar or cool place. Take *a stag's heart* and cut off the fat, cut it very small and pour on it as much white wine as will cover it. Let it stand all night covered in a cool place and the next day add to it the before mentioned ingredients, mixing the whole well together and adding a *pint of the best rose water, and a pint of the juice of celandine.* Put the whole into a glass still and raise it well, in order to keep in the steam broth of the still and receiver. When it is drawn off put it into bottles, cork them well, set them in a cool place, and the water will keep good for a considerable time.

Home brewed beer was something they did as an everyday chore in the country where there were no Inns and only a couple of cottages miles from the nearest town.

W. & J. BURROW,

3, Mark Lane Square, Great Tower Street, London, E.C.

(and at GREAT MALVERN,)

Manufacturers of IRON WINE BINS, MINERAL WATER RACKS, and every requisite for the use of Wine Merchants, Hotel Keepers, Restaurant Proprietors, Distillers, Brewers, &c.

Patentees of the "Slider" Wine Bin, of one, two, and three bottles deep.

Porcelain Bin Labels, with name of various wines.

SHERRY

and

Bin Numbers, from 1 to 300.

60

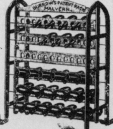

Double Slider Bin for 12 dozens. A variety of sizes kept in Stock both with and without doors.

Brass Pipe Forcer.

Seltzer or Soda Rack for 6 dozen Bottles, for Cellars, Shops, Hotels, Wine Offices, &c. All sizes kept in Stock.

Pewter and Copper Measures.

Pot Stretchers.

Bar Spirit Cocks, Brass or Plated.

Funnels of every Description.

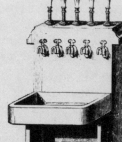

Pewter Pots of all the usual patterns.

SHERRY

Porcelain Casks of Various Designs.

Beer Engines, from Three to Eight Pulls.

Mullers made to order.

Illustrated Catalogues with Prices on Application.

Wine bins and beer engines etc. (*The Caterer* 1878)

165. Directions for Brewing in Cottages

1 peck of malt, 2ozs of hops, 6 gallons of water, a few birch twigs, or a little wheat straw, and 1 cupful of yeast.

Boil 3 gallons of water, take it off as soon as it boils, and let it stand till you can see your face in it. While the water is heating get ready a clean rinsing tub with a small hole bored in the bottom, and stopped with a peg or cork. Cover it with a few birch twigs or some clean wheat straw, put a coarse bit of cloth over the bottom of the tub, then put in the malt. Pour the water on it, and stir it well for a few minutes.

Cover it close with a sack and let it stand for 3 days to keep warm near the fire, then pull out the peg or cork, and let the whole run into a bucket. Put the peg back again immediately, and having prepared another 3 gallons of water just as you did before, pour it on the malt and set it by the fire as before, covered close for 2 hours. As soon as you have emptied the second 3 gallons of water out of the boiler put into it the first run from the malt, and boil it a ¼ an hour with the hops.

Strain it through a sieve into a shallow vessel to cool as quickly as possible. Run off the second 3 gallons, and boil them with the same hops for an half hour, then strain and cool as for the first run. Mix both runs from the malt together, add a small teacupful of yeast, and let it ferment for two or three days, during which time it must be frequently skimmed. Three pints of nice yeast will thus be obtained. When the fermentation is over, put the beer in a small cask, where it will probably ferment a little, after which stop it down close.

Today we can buy a homebrew kit for a few pounds, but the satisfaction from doing it the old traditional way must have been wonderful.

166. Mulled Ale

2 pints of old ale, 1¾ inch cinnamon stick ground, 1 teaspoon of brown sugar, 2 crushed bay leaves, 1 small piece of root ginger crushed in a muslin bag, 1 whole lemon sliced thinly.

Place all the ingredients in a large saucepan and bring to the boil. Remove the muslin. This will be a bit difficult for the housewife today if she does not have a coal fire. For we now need a poker white-hot to plunge into the pan until the bubbling stops. Then serve in glasses after the heated ale cools.

162

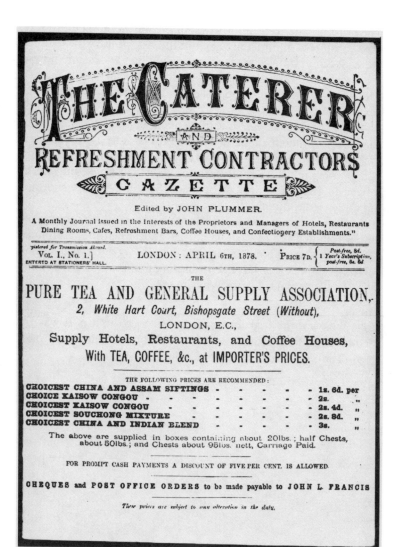

Tea and Coffee Suppliers (*The Caterer* 1878).

Tea and Coffee

The most popular refreshing drink of the day in this country is tea, now considered almost a necessity of life. Previous to the middle of the 17th century it was not used in England, and it was unknown to the Greeks and Romans. Pepys said, from his diary — "September 25th 1661 — I sent for a cup of tea (a China drink), of which I had never drunk before."

Two years later it was so rare a commodity in England that the English East India Company bought 2lbs of it as a present for his Majesty. In 1666 it was sold in London for 60 shillings a pound. Tea growing in China dates back to prehistoric times, but was not started in India and Sri Lanka until 1865. We import enormous quantities from India.

Coffee was hardly known in Europe before the 17th century. The Dutch founded the East India coffee trade when they introduced coffee into Java about 1685. Brazil is the greatest producer of coffee. Instant coffee was the invention of an Englishman who was living in Guatemala, Mr G. Washington.

Cocoa

Columbus was the first European to see cocoa in use. It was first used in England in 1650. It was not sold for eating until Victoria's reign. The first being made by Cadbury's

Chapter 39
Victorian Advice on Diet

In 1875 George Overend Drewry M.D. wrote a book called *Common Sense Management of the Stomach* which I found very interesting. The Victorians were very conscious about their weight, but all this considered there were very few men over 5' 6" tall and the majority of men had a figure comparable with that of Mr Pickwick. The women had bosoms that were over 50" and anything less than that was considered small.

Read this passage from *The Stomach of Youth* and you will know why:—

The Food of Youth
1. The quantity must necessarily depend upon the individual requirements of each case, and the amount of wear and tear of tissue in exercise undergone. The quality must be as nutritious, light and wholesome, and unstimulating as possible, and the diet essentially of a mixed character. Meat once or twice a day, with plenty of vegetables, light farinaceous puddings, with plenty of eggs and milk, and above all, the basin of oatmeal porridge for breakfast and supper every day. This, as I have before said, must be boiled and stirred for half to three quarters of an hour, and eaten when the boiling has converted the starch into an assimilable form, with a pint of new milk, with or without a little butter added to the porridge, and salt in preference to sugar. Whatever else is eaten in the day, the porridge must be insisted upon; the health that it imparts, the muscle that it develops, are incredible, if not witnessed, as it has been by myself; and let me say, doctors will not have much to do when the infectious diseases are stamped out, as they will surely be by isolation, disinfection, ventilation, drainage, and pure water supply, and when every man, woman, and child above two years of age fill their stomachs twice a day with oatmeal porridge.

   For drink, a glass of light bitter ale or porter at luncheon or dinner may be allowed, but wine should never be given, unless specially ordered; it is unnecessary and heating. A full meal of solid food should never be taken later than four hours before bedtime; the porridge may be taken anytime, as it is easily digested during sleep, and forms a bland and comforting meal. The hour for bed should be fixed as early as possible, and rising in the morning should be correspondingly early. All water drunk should be boiled and filtered, and a mattress should always be used to sleep on: time enough for a feather bed and down pillows when aching limbs require their soft support; for young people they are enervating and objectionable.

   The cold bath, which I have pointed out is a matter of the highest importance for girls, is no less so for boys, who should have a shower or sponge bath every morning, and swim in a large bath, or better the sea, as often as practicable; for this purpose every boy ought to be taught to swim as early as possible, and at the same time he ought to be taught that there is as much pleasure and benefit to be obtained by swimming in five feet of water as in fifty, and that to risk life wantonly by swimming far out of depth is not courage, but foolhardiness, which frequently meets with the punishment it deserves.

2. Beginning, then, with breakfast, I would recommend a basin of oatmeal porridge to everyone. I wish most particularly to impress upon my readers the value of oatmeal porridge, if not in the morning and evening, at least in the morning, as a nutrient, an emollient to the coats of the stomach, and a laxative to the bowels. I may say that in some forms of dyspepsia it is indispensable and in all cases is far superior to bread and milk. After a pint or more of oatmeal porridge has been taken, a little game, fish, bacon, eggs etc., with coffee, tea or cocoa, as preferred, may be taken, and will enable most persons to make a very satisfactory and wholesome meal. The time should be about eight or nine o'clock a.m. after which nothing more is requisite until one or two p.m. when luncheon, in the shape of bread and cheese and a glass of ale, basin of soup, and glass of sherry, or chop with or without vegetables, will enable most people in tolerable health to last until dinner time. In the case of invalids, the middle of the day is the best time for dinner, and they often require an egg beaten up with a little sherry or brandy and water, a biscuit and glass of wine, or a basin of broth or soup, in the interval between breakfast and dinner. They also require a lighter and more fluid kind of diet than the robust, who, when in full exercise, can eat and drink almost anything with comparative impunity.

3. As I have before pointed out, one kind of aliment is not sufficient; meat therefore which represents the nitrogenous element of diet, by no means forms a proper food by itself, and requires the starch element, which is so well supplied by the potato, upon which principally, with the addition of milk, and occasionally with a litle bacon or fish, so many thousands of human beings thrive. Other vegetables of all kinds, if not absolutely necessary, are highly beneficial and wholesome. Many persons who entertain a mistaken idea, that they cannot eat vegetables, would be much benefited by their use; and without wishing to attach undue importance to the eating of vegetables, it is my duty to point out that they form part, and an important part, of man's daily food; but it in no way follows that because they play an important part in conjunction with animal food, they can be used with benefit solely as a diet of themselves, any more than meat can without vegetables. One error is as egregious as the other, whether it be all vegetables or all meat. Bread furnishes in another form the same kind of food as the potato; and in cases where potatoes are not liked, bread and flour of various kinds, in puddings, etc., make up the deficiency, and form a heathy food.
It is absolutely necessary for the well being of the body, that nitrogenous food, as exemplified in meat, starchy food, as in bread, potatoes, all kinds of farinaceous puddings etc., and carbonaceous foods, as in fat, oil, grease, butter etc., and vegetables or fruit, shall form part of our daily food. A certain amount of sugar may also be taken with benefit,

except in certain cases of deranged function, in which sugar speedily produces acidity, when of course it must be avoided.

Salt is a highly necessary addition to a wholesome diet, furnishing as it does that most important acid of digestion, the hydrochloric which cannot possibly be supplied in any way as readily as by salt. It may be accepted therefore as a fact, that salt is an absolute necessity as an article of wholesome diet, in conjunction with animal and vegetable food. Large quantities of salt meat, without such vegetables, will produce an eruptive disease called scurvy, which in former times used to be very common in the navy, but which was cured by the use of plenty of vegetables and unsalted meat.

Fish furnishes us not only with a very agreeable change in diet, but also, being rich in phosphatic food, is a direct benefit in contributing that element of the organism on which, in combination with lime, the solidity of our bones depends, and which influences by its presence the condition of the nerves generally.

The amount of mixed food necessary to maintain health varies with the individual power of assimilation; that is, the power, after absorption has taken place, of the different organs and structures of the body to assimilate the nutritive elements contained in the food, and to form fresh structures of each kind from it. It is also very dependent on the amount of wear and tear of the system daily to be borne. These important facts must be kept in constant remembrance, if health is to be maintained. As it is impossible to adjust exactly the supply and the demand, the safe plan is to err on the side of exercise, and not of idleness. Then, if a surplus quantity of meat or drink is taken, it is readily disposed of, and not much harm results.

Isn't it interesting to note that a vegetarian diet was disapproved of and also, as now, lots of exercise is recommended to keep you in good health.

Chapter 40
Salads

Salads are a very popular summer dish and a vegetarian's paradise. In the beginning, our Saxon ancestors' gardens had radish, parsley, mustard, cress, mint, spinach, onions, coriander, rosemary, fennel, chervil and also mushrooms.

Salat *(The forme of Cury* 1385)
> 'Take Psel, Sawge, garlee, chiboli, oynons, leek, borage, mynt poneet, fenel, and ton tressis (cresses), rew, roemarye Purslarye, laue, and waische hem clene, pike hem, pluk he small wip phu (thine) hand and myng hem wel with rawe oile, lay on vyneg and salt and sue it forth.

*To make a Salad (*ascribed to the Rev Sydney Smith 1755)
> Two boiled potatoes strained through a kitchen sieve,
> Softness and smoothness to the salad give;
> Of mordant mustard take a single spoon,
> Distrust the condiment that bites too soon;
> Yet deem it not, thou man of taste, a fault,
> To add a double quantity of salt.
> Four times the spoon with oil of Lucca crown,
> And twice with vinegar, procured from town;
> True taste requires it, and your poet begs,
> The pounded yellow of two well boiled eggs,
> Let onions' atoms lurk within the bowl,
> And scarce suspected animate the whole;
> And lastly, in the flavoured compound toss,
> A magic spoonful of anchovy sauce;
> Oh, great and glorious! oh, herbaceous meat!
> T'would tempt the dying anchoret to eat;
> Back to the world he'd turn his weary soul,
> And dip his finger in the salad bowl.

167. Lobster Salad (1868)

One hen lobster, lettuces, endive, mustard and cress, radishes, beetroot, cucumber, some hard boiled eggs.

Pour the salad mixture into the bowl, wash and dry the lettuces and endive, and cut them fine with a silver knife. Add them to the dressing, with the pickings from the body of the lobster, and part of the meat from the shell cut into small pieces. Rub the yolks of two or three hard boiled eggs through a sieve, and afterwards the coral of the lobster, then place the salad very lightly in the bowl, and garnish it with the coral, yolks of the hard boiled eggs sliced beetroot, cucumber, radishes, and the pieces of lobster. Place as a border hard boiled eggs cut across, with the delicate leaves of the celery and endive between them.

168. Salad (Bohemia) Mary Jewry (1868)

Take the yolk of one or two raw eggs, according to the size of the salad you require, beat them up well, *add a little salt and mustard,* and chop *two young onions, or leeks* about the size of grass, then add *the oil and vinegar,* and beat the whole up into a thick sauce. Cut in the salad, and put *thin slices of beetroot* at the top. Sprinkle *a little salt* over it and do not stir it up until the moment you use it. For a small salad three dessertspoonfuls of oil, and one of vinegar will do.

169. Summer Salad (1856)

Three lettuces, a good quantity of mustard and cress, some young radishes, boiled beetroot, hard boiled eggs.

Wash and carefully remove the decayed leaves from the lettuces and mustard and cress, drain them well from the water, and cut them and the radishes into small pieces with a silver knife; arrange them lightly on a dish with the mustard and cress mixed with them (and any salad dressing you prefer with them)

Garnish with boiled beetroot, *cucumbers,* and hard boiled eggs cut into slices with *some vegetable flowers.*

Slices of cold poultry, or flaked fish, may be added to a summer salad, and are extremely good.

169

170. Salade de légumes Escoffier (1859)

Carrots, turnips, potatoes, French beans, peas, asparagus tips, sprigs of cauliflower, oil and vinegar dressing, chopped parsley, chopped chervil.

Cut equal quantities of carrots, turnips and potatoes into small squares (diced). Prepare the same quantity of French beans, fresh peas, asparagus tips, cut into small pieces, and sprigs of cauliflower.

Arrange in separate heaps on the serving dish. Pour the dressing over and sprinkle with the parsley and chervil.

Oil and vinegar can be used with all salads in the proportion of 3 parts oil to 1 part vinegar with the addition of a little English mustard, salt and freshly ground pepper.

Chapter 41
Preserving Food

Food-canning was a direct response to the needs of the French Revolution. In 1809 Nicholas Appert, the French chef, won the 1st prize of 12,000 francs for his method of heated jars in food preservation. Tin canning was introduced in London by Mr Peter Durand. He sold his patent to Donkin, Hall and Gamble who set up a Preservatory in Bermondsey, London around 1830. It was not until Louis Pasteur (1822 – 95) that the canning process became hygienically safe (in about 1861). The cans were all hand-made up to 1865. That was one of the reasons why canned food was more expensive than fresh. It was mainly bought by the Navy, explorers and the Army to whom convenient, preserved foods were of great importance. Canned meats were not popular at all. The meat that they canned in Deptford in the 1860s was named 'Sweet Fanny Adams' an expression that is still heard today. The name was immortalised when Frederick Baker in 1867 murdered a woman named Fanny Adams, after which he hacked her into small pieces. He was hanged at Winchester Gaol on Christmas Eve of that year. It was the soldiers that named the meat after her. When they were asked at the cookhouse 'what's for tea' the reply would be 'Sweet Fanny Adams'.

Because of airfreight and modern refrigerated transportation, better production techniques and supplies from developing countries, seasons of various foods have now been considerably extended, I am very happy to say.

Fruits

Apples	all year round
Apricot	May to September
Blackberry	autumn
Cherry	May to July
Cranberry	November to January
Damsons	September to October
Gooseberry	Summer
Grapes	all year round
Greengage	August to September
Melon	May to October best (can be got all year round)

Nectarine	June to September
Peach	all the year round
Pineapple	all the year round (you could not say that 15 years ago)
Plum	July to October
Raspberry	Summer
Rhubarb	January to July
Strawberry	June to September (best July to August)

Seasonal fruit and vegetables can now be frozen for use all year round.

The Victorians could not freeze them so they would bottle them for the winter. Fresh fruit such as currants, raspberries, cherries, gooseberries, plums of all kinds and damsons just before they were ripe, they would gather them when it was a nice dry day. Pick off the stalks without bruising or breaking the skins and reject any that were at all blemished.

If they gathered them in the damp weather the fruit would go mouldy, if it was not gathered properly. They would have ready some perfectly DRY glass bottles, and new soft corks or bungs. They would burn a match in each bottle, to exhaust the air, and quickly place in the fruit to be preserved, gently cork the bottles and put them into a very cool oven. Where the fruit would shrink by about ¼. They would then take the bottles out and immediately beat the corks in tight, cut the tops off, and cover them with melted resin. If they were kept in a dry place they would keep for months.

Time: 6 hours in a very slow oven.

Chapter 42
Jams, Chutneys, Jellies and Pickles

Jam making is a pleasant occupation and not difficult provided certain rules are carefully followed.

Weighing and measuring must be absolutely accurate, and the jam must be boiled till a good set is secured. A common failing of home-made jams is that they are too runny.

The best sort of preserving pan to use is a strong copper pan or aluminium. Never fill it too full or the jam may boil over.

Either loaf, granulated or preserving sugar can be used for jam. Always use the best fruit. And finally the jars should be scrupulously clean. The Victorians used to swop jams for all types of homemade produce, and sell them at local fairs and exhibitions. Jams will keep perfectly for a year if stored in a cool, dry place.

171. Blackberry & Apple Jam *The Good Housekeeper* 1845
8lb blackberries, 12lb Sugar and 4lbs of cooking apples.
Peel and core the apples and slice them rather coarsely. Stalk the blackberries and put them with the apples in the preserving pan. Add the sugar and heat slowly till it is dissolved, *stirring all the time. Then bring to the boil and let it continue boiling till the jam will set when tested. Skim if necessary. Always let the jam cool a little before pouring into the jars, and make sure the jars are also warm.*

172. Cherry Jam *The Frugal Housewife* 1811
6lb black cherries, 2lb red currants, 6lb sugar and a little water.
Stone the cherries, wash the red currants. Boil the red currants, adding a little water. When they have boiled for ½ hour strain them through a jelly bag and add the juice to the cherries. Boil the cherries and juice for ½ hour until the cherries are soft. Add the sugar and bring to the boil slowly, allowing the sugar to melt before it boils. Boil quickly until the juices are thick and not too runny.

173. **Rhubarb Jam** Author's recipe
3lbs rhubarb (cut up), 3lbs sugar, 1½ozs root ginger and 2 small lemons.

Cut the rhubarb into small pieces (½ inch) and put it into a preserving pan with the sugar. Heat slowly till the sugar is dissolved, *stirring all the time.* Add the lemon juice and finely grated rind; bruise the ginger, tie it in a muslin bag and add it also. Boil till the mixture sets when tested, skimming if necessary. Remove the ginger and pour the jam into WARM jars.

174. **Lemon Curd** Mary Jewry 1860
6 lemons, 6 eggs, 6ozs butter, 18ozs castor sugar.

Place the butter in a large stone jam jar and stand it in a saucepan ¾ full of water. Let the water boil. Sieve the sugar on to a piece of paper. Grate the yellow part of the rind on to a plate. Squeeze the lemon juice into a small basin. Beat the eggs together in another basin. When the butter is melted add the sugar, then the lemon juice and rind, and finally the eggs. Stir over the boiling water without stopping till the mixture becomes thick (½ hour). Pour it into the warm jars and tie down as soon as it is cold.

175. **Tangerine Marmalade**
12 tangerines, 3 lemons, sugar and water.

Remove the lemon rinds and slice up the lemons. Pare the tangerines very thinly and shred up the peel. Then slice up the insides and put them with the shredded peel and the lemons into a basin. Cover the fruit with cold water, allowing 2½ pints to every 1lb fruit, and let it soak for 24 hours.

Put all the pips in a separate basin with a little water. The next day strain them and add the liquid to the fruit and water. Boil the mixture for ½ hour and let it stand again for 24 hours.

Then add the sugar, allowing ¾lb to every pint of pulp. Dissolve the sugar slowly, stirring well, and then boil quickly till the juice will set into a jelly when tested. Skim and put into warm jars. It might have taken 3 days to make but I am sure the family will be pleased at the end result.

176. Apple Chutney
6lbs peeled & cored apples, 3lb sultanas, 4½lbs demerara sugar, 3oz mustard seeds, 3lb shallots, ¼lb salt, ¾ozs cayenne pepper and 4 pints vinegar.

Chop up the apples and shallots. Place all the ingredients in a pan together and boil them until thick, about 2½ hours, stirring and watching that it does not catch. Pour the mixture into the jars when warm, and fix down the tops tight.

177. Piccalilli (Lancashire recipe 1873)
2lbs of cauliflower, cucumbers, button onions, french beans, 4 chillies, a little ground ginger, 1oz flour, 1½ pints of vinegar, 1oz turmeric, 1oz mustard and 2ozs sugar.

Prepare 2lbs of the above vegetables. The cauliflower should be broken up into small pieces, using only the flower. Choose only small beans and string them only. Peel the onions but leave them whole. Peel the cucumbers and cut into good size pieces. Spread all the vegetables out on a big dish and sprinkle them with salt. Let them stand for 12 hours.

Then drain them well and leave them to dry. Mix the mustard and flour to a smooth paste with a little vinegar. Put the rest of the vinegar on to boil with the turmeric, chillies, ground ginger and sugar. Then add the mustard paste, stirring it well. When it boils put in all the vegetables and boil gently for 10 minutes. When cool, bottle the piccalilli, and tie down when cold.

178. Tomato Chutney (Workman's pickle 1854)
3lb very ripe tomatoes, 3lb peeled & cored apples, 1lb sultanas, 1lb raisins, 1½lb brown sugar, 1½lb small onions, 2 teaspoons cayenne pepper, 4 teaspoons salt, 20 cloves, 10 chillies, 3 pints of vinegar.

Place the tomatoes in hot water and remove the skins. Chop up finely the tomatoes, apples, raisins and onions. Put all the ingredients, except the vinegar, in a pan and simmer for ½ hour. Add the vinegar and simmer for 3 hours. Pour the mixture into the jars and tie down while hot.

179. Apple Jelly Author's recipe
4lbs cooking apples, 2ozs root ginger, 2lb sugar.

Cut up the apples, just cover with water, and in a little muslin hang the root ginger. Bring to the boil, and simmer gently for 1 hour until fruit is quite soft. Strain through a fine sieve and leave to go cold. To every pint of juice allow 1lb of sugar. Bring to the boil and cook rapidly until the jelly sets.

180. Damson Jam Author's recipe

3lb Damsons, 3lb Sugar, and 1 pint of water.
Wash the fruit, add the water and bring slowly to the boil in a preserving pan. Simmer until the damsons are cooked and soft. Add the sugar, stir till dissolved and bring slowly to the boil. Boil very quickly and remove the stones as they rise to the top. Pot and cover while hot.

181. Medlar Jelly (1868)

This was a very popular fruit that tasted like wine when ripe and soft, and was often seen on the great tables of the 19th century. You can still buy this fruit from your greengrocer.
4lb of Medlars (ripe), water to cover and ¾lb preserving sugar to every pint of liquor.
Wash the ripe medlars, put them in a pan and cover them with water. Simmer very slowly until they become a pulp. Strain them through a very fine sieve and leave them for 24 hours. Then put them into a preserving pan, allowing ¾lb sugar to every pint of juice. Bring to the boil and boil rapidly until it sets when tested. Pot and cover.

182. Mint Jelly Author's recipe

This being one of the nicer accompaniments to new potatoes and fresh baby lamb.
4lb of cooking apples, 1 pint of water, 6 tablespoons of fresh mint leaves, 1 cup of tarragon vinegar 8fl ozs, sugar 1lb to every 1lb of juice, and 5 drops of green food colouring.
Put the sliced apples into the preserving pan and add the water with half the mint leaves and bring to the boil. Simmer for 50 minutes then add the vinegar and boil for a further 7 minutes. Strain through a jelly bag or muslin, and let it cool for 14 hours. Measure the juice and add 1lb of sugar to each pint of juice. Return the pan with the sugar and juice, stir until dissolved. Bring back to boil until setting point then add the mint and food colouring, skim and stir well before potting.

183. Lemon Pickle (1804)

Take about *a score of lemons,* grate off the out rinds very thin and cut them into quarters, but leave the bottoms whole. Rub on them equally *half a pound of bay salt* and spread them on a large pewter dish. Either put them in a cool oven or let them dry gradually by the fire, till the juice is all dried into the peels; then put them into a well glazed pitcher, with *an ounce of mace and half an ounce of cloves* beat fine, *an ounce of nutmeg* cut into thin slices, *four ounces of garlic* peeled, *half a pint of mustard seed* bruised a little, and tied in a muslin bag. Pour upon them *two quarts of boiling white wine vinegar,* close the pitcher well up, and let it stand five or six days by the fire. Shake it well up every day, then tie it close, and let it stand for three months to take off the bitter. When you bottle it put the pickle and lemon into a hair sieve, press them well to get out the liquor, and let it stand till another day; then pour off the fine and bottle it. Let the other stand three or four days and it will refine itself. Pour it off and bottle it; let it stand again, and bottle it till the whole is refined. It may be put into any white sauce and will not hurt the colour. It is very good for fish sauce and made dishes. One teaspoonful is enough for white, and two for brown sauce for a fowl. It is a most useful pickle and gives a pleasant flavour. Always put it in before you thicken the sauce, or put any cream in, lest the sharpness should make it curdle.

Chapter 43
Household Tips

The servants of the household had plenty of work to do, and the useful household hints below came in very handy. They made their own blacking for the boots, furniture polish, tooth powder and the Eau-de-Cologne to cover the smell of the other dirty jobs they had to do. Here are some of those old Victorian recipes that we would not even dream of making today.

To Clean Chimney Pieces
Equal quantities of soft soap and pearl-ash. Put the soap and pearl-ash on the chimney piece with a soft flannel, let it lie on the marble for a few minutes. Wash it off with warm water, not too hot, then wash with cold spring water.

To Cement Broken China
Beat *lime* to a very fine almost invisible dust, sift it through book muslin. Then tie it up in a piece of thin muslin as powdered starch is sometimes used. Brush some *white of egg* over the edges of the china, dust the lime rapidly over them, put the edges together and tie a string round the cup, leave till it is firm. *Isinglass* (gelatine) dissolved in *spirits of wine,* in proportion of 1oz to 2 wine glassfuls of the spirit, is also a good cement.

Removing Paint from Wood
Mix *1 pound of washing soda* with *2 pounds of unslacked lime,* and if the paint is very strong on the wood *add ½lb of potash.* Mix these ingredients together, and dilute with water until the mixture becomes rather thicker than whitewash. Now rub it on with a piece of wood folded in a rag. The person who uses this must be careful not to touch it with their hands.

Table Polish

½ pint of spirits of wine, 1½oz of gum shellac, ½oz gum benzoin and ½oz gum sandarac.
Put the whole in a bottle for a day or two and shake it a few times. When the gums are dissolved it is fit for use. When the polish is laid on thick enough, take a clean wad and cloth, put a little clean spirit of wine on the wad, the same as you did with the polish, rub it the same way but very lightly and until quite dry. You must then put a little oil on the cloth, and rub as in laying on the polish.

To Make Blacking

4ozs of ivory black, 3ozs of treacle, a tablespoonful of sweet oil, 1½ pints of beer, and 1oz of sulphuric acid. Mix with a spoonful of sweet oil the 4ozs of black ivory and the 3ozs of black treacle, pour on it by degrees a pint and half of beer. Stir it well together and then pour in 1oz of sulphuric acid, keeping it till the effervescence ceases, bottle it, and it may be used immediately.

To Make Lace String-coloured

2 tablespoons of soot, cover with *a pint of boiling water,* and leave it standing for ¾ hour, then strain through a muslin. After washing the lace, dip it in this, stretch it out on a covered board to dry.

Shampoo for the Hair

½oz of glycerine, ½oz of spirit of rosemary and 5ozs water mixed well together and shaken.

Shampoo to make your Hair Smell Nice

½lb of hogs lard, a wineglass of rose-water, a teaspoonful of ammonia, scented with jessamine or any other scent you prefer, mix well together and bottle.

A Winter Soap for Chapped or Rough Hands

3lbs of common yellow soap, 1oz of camphor dissolved in 1oz of rose and 1oz lavender water. Beat the yellow soap and the camphor dissolved in the rose and lavender water in a mortar until it becomes a paste. Make it into balls to dry, and set it in a cool place for the winter. The best time to make it is in the spring.

Tooth Powder

¼oz of boll ammoniac, ¼oz of bark, ¼oz of powdered camphor and a ¼oz of powdered myrrh. Mix all the ingredients very thoroughly together. All tooth powders should be kept in a tight fitting wooden box.

Carr's Ladder Tapes.

USEFUL HINTS.

Cleaning Ceilings.—Ceilings that look very rough and manifest a tendency to peel should be gone over with a solution of 1 oz. alum to 1 quart water. This will remove the superfluous lime and render the ceiling white.

To keep Lemons Fresh.—Place them in a jar with water enough to cover them. They will keep fresh this way several days without changing the water. They will also keep fresh if not placed in the sunshine or exposed to much heat.

To make Tough Beef Tender.—Cut the steaks the day before using into slices about two inches thick, rub them over with a small quantity of soda, wash off next morning, cut into suitable thickness, and cook to notion. It is said to answer very well.

Knife-handle Cement.—Cutlers' cement, for fastening blades of dinner-knives in ivory handles, consists of rosin four parts, beeswax one part, plaster of Paris or brickdust one part. Fill the hole in the handle with the cement, heat the tang of the blade, then press it in.

Rancid Butter.—To sweeten rancid butter it is recommended to wash it, first in fresh milk, and afterwards in an abundance of fresh water. The *rationale* of the process is that the milk absorbs the butyric and other fatty acids to the development of which are due the unpleasant smell and taste of old butter.

French Table Mustard.—The following recipe for *Moutarde à la Ravigote* is said to be excellent. It is much used in France. Take two ounces each of parsley, chervil, and cives; one ounce each of cloves, garlic, thyme, and tarragon; eight ounces of salt; four ounces of olive oil; four quarts of vinegar; and the required quantity of common mustard, in powder. Cut or contuse the plants and spices, and macerate them for fifteen days in the vinegar, strain the liquid through a coarse cloth, and add to it the other ingredients, so as to obtain twelve quarts of mustard. The tarragon should not be left out of the preparation, for it is one of the most pleasant aromatics for culinary purposes.

To Banish Rats.—A restaurant proprietor informs us that he has succeeded in getting rid of rats on his premises by using hardwood ashes mixed with as little water as would stick them together. A good supply of wet ashes should be placed in the holes, so that the rats cannot run in or out without passing through it. The wet ashes burn their feet, and to relieve the pain they lick them. This burns their tongues and lips, and as they do not approve of such inhospitable treatment, they forthwith shift their quarters. The rats appear to have the facility of communicating with each other, so the first rat treated that way tells his friends, who very wisely take up their residence in the next house or barn, as the case may be.

Chemical Tests.—As the fees of the analytical chemist are beyond the means of many, a few simple test papers, says Mr. Watson, might be prepared and used for many purposes. Certain cards should be prepared and hung in closets, which by changing colour would immediately betray the presence of sewer gas in the atmosphere. Other papers might be prepared for testing the purity of water or tea or other articles of daily consumption. The paper for testing water would immediately, should lead be present, betray its existence; the papers for testing tea would betray the presence of copper, and so forth. The papers might be prepared in packets and labelled. These test papers would be very inexpensive, and could be used by the most inexperienced with confidence.

Preserving Potatoes.—The following is the way this is done in Lubeck. The potatoes are peeled by hand, and cut into discs by a machine. These are put into a basket, and this into a boiler, where the potatoes are nearly, but not quite, boiled. The discs are next put on wire frames in a dry oven, where they are dried quite hard. It is important to preserve the colour of the potatoes; and to prevent their turning grey, as they would by the above process alone, the material, after slicing, is treated with cold water, to which has been added one per cent. of sulphuric acid, or one or two per cent. of muriatic acid. Then it is washed in pure water, and the drying proceeds. The preparation obtained, which has lost none of its starch, is of a slightly citron-yellow tint, and transparent like gum. Boiled with water and a little salt, it is said to resume the natural colour and fibrous structure of potatoes, and is not distinguishable in taste from the newly-boiled vegetable.

REMOVING STAINS.

THE following recipes, partly from the *Apothek Zeitung*, will be found useful in the removal of stains from table covers, napkins, and other textile articles.

Acids, Vinegar, Orange Juice, etc.—White cottons and linens, wash with pure water, or warm water, to which a little chlorine has been added; for coloured goods or silks use ammonia, diluted according to the fineness of the tissue, and the delicacy of the colour.

Fruit.—White cotton or linen, use the fumes of burning sulphur, or warm chlorine water; coloured cottons or woollens, tepid soapsuds or ammonia; silk, tepid soapsuds or ammonia, very gentle rubbing. The labour of removal is rendered easier if directly a stain is made it is covered with some common table salt, which absorbs a considerable portion of the stain, leaving a less quantity to be removed.

Grease Spots.—If in white linen or cotton goods, use soap or weak soda solution; coloured calico, warm soapsuds; woollens, soapsuds or diluted ammonia; silks, benzine, ether, ammonia, magnesia, chalk, yolk of egg, diluted with warm water.

Lime, Lye, Alkalies.—White cottons and linens should be washed with cold water; for coloured goods and silks, a weak solution of citric acid applied with the tip of the finger to the spot, previously moistened with water, will be found effectual.

Ordinary Writing Ink, or Rust.—White cottons and linens require a warm solution of oxalic acid, or dilute hydrochloric acid; coloured cottons and woollens, repeated washings with a solution of citric acid; if the colour be fast, ink cannot be removed from silk without injury to the appearance or texture.

Paint, Varnish, or Resin.—For white or coloured cotton and woollen goods, use turpentine or benzine, followed by soapsuds; silk goods, benzine, ether, soap, but hard rubbing must be avoided.

Stearin or Sperm.—Use spirits of wine, whatever the fabric, in the proportion of ninety-five parts to five of water.

Walnut Shells.—For white cottons and linens, use either chlorinated solution of soda, warm chlorine water, or concentrated solution of tartaric acid; coloured goods or silks, chlorine diluted with warm water, according to the tissue, and its colour, each application to be followed with washing with water.

Wine, Beer, etc.—Same as for fruit-stains.

Tar, Axle-grease.—White cottons or linens require soap, oil of turpentine and water, each applied by turns; coloured cottons and woollens, first smear with lard, rub with soap and water, and let it stand for a short time; then wash with oil of turpentine and water alternately; silks, the same, using benzine instead of turpentine, and dropping the water from a certain height on the under side of the stain. Rubbing must be avoided.

Stains of blood, sugar, gelatine, and albumen may be removed by simply washing in warm water. In all cases where the stain is not of a greasy nature, the use of salt as an absorbent will be found advisable.

Miss de Rothschild's Bridecake.—The wedding cake which stood on the breakfast-table at the marriage party of Lord Rosebery was manufactured by Messrs. Bolland and Sons, the celebrated bridecake manufacturers, of Chester. It was built in three tiers, and weighed about one hundred weight. The lowest tier was wreathed with flowers, and adorned with birds beautifully modelled; the second was decorated with medallions of silk painted with orange blossoms and cornucopias; the third tier was festooned with flowers. Each tier had an ornamental gallery of sugar work, and the top was surmounted with a lovely vase of flowers.

Useful Hints (*The Caterer* 1878).

Cartwright's Prescription for Toothache
A little *ether and laudanum* mixed, and applied on wool to the tooth. I strongly recommend a visit to the dentist instead.

Writing Ink (marking)
1 drachm and a half of lunar caustic, 1 scruple of sap green, 6 drachms of water, 2 drachms of mucilage. And *Preparation Liquor; ½oz of salt of tartar or subcarbonate of potash, ½oz of mucilage, ½oz of water.*
The preparation is to be put on with a small brush, and when it is nearly dry, smooth the surface by means of a spoon or glass. After which use the marking ink.

Bouquet de Victoria
1oz of essence of bergamot, ½ a drachm of oil of cloves, 3 drachms of oil of lavender, 6 grains of grain musk, ½ drachm of aromatic vinegar, 1½ pints of wine spirits. Mix well and distil.

Eau-de-Cologne
1 drachm of orange-flower, 1 drachm of essence of citron, 4ozs of essence of mellisse, 1oz of cidret, 1oz of rosemary, 3ozs of bergamot, 1oz lavender, 1oz musk and 4 pints of rectified spirits of wine.
When the chemist has mixed the essences, put them into 2 quart bottles of recitified spirits of wine, but care must be taken that potash is not used by the chemist to melt the essences as it burns. Entire cost in 1860 1/6d

Pot Pourri
½lb of bay-salt, a ¼lb of saltpetre bruised with *a little common salt.* Then add to it *threepennyworth of cloves pounded, the same of storax, 1 small nutmeg grated, 3 bay leaves broken, lavender flower freshly gathered, rose leaves gathered dry* and added without drying to the above mixture.

Chapter 44
Pot Dishes

When potting be sure to make it a rule that whatever article you do is well covered with *clarified butter* before you send it to the oven. Tie it close with strong paper, and let it be well baked. When it comes from the oven, pick every bit of skin you can and drain away the gravy, otherwise the article potted will be apt to turn sour. Beat your seasoning very fine and spread it on gradually. Before you put it into your pot press it well and before you put on the clarified butter let it be perfectly cold.

184. Potting Venison

Rub your venison all over with *red wine;* season it with *beaten mace, pepper and salt;* put it into an earthen dish and pour over it half a pint of red wine, and *a pound of butter* and then send it to the oven. If it be a shoulder put *a coarse paste* over it, and let it lie in the oven all night. When it comes out pick the meat clean from the bones and beat it in a marble mortar with the fat from your gravy. If you find it not sufficiently seasoned add more with clarified butter and keep beating it till it becomes like a fine paste. Then press it hard down into your pots, pour clarified butter over it and keep it in a dry place.

185. Potting Beef (1816)

Take *half a pound of brown sugar and an ounce of salt petre and rub it into twelve pounds of beef.* Let it lie twenty four hours; then wash it clean and dry it well with a cloth. Season it to your taste with *pepper, salt and mace* and cut it into five or six pieces. Put it into an earthen pot, with *a pound of butter* in lumps on it, set it in a hot oven and let it stand three hours, then take it out, cut off the hard outsides and beat it in a mortar. Add to it a little more pepper, salt and mace. Then oil a pound of butter in the gravy and fat that came from your beef and put it in as you find necesary; but beat the meat very fine. Then put it into your pot, press it close down, pour clarified butter over it, and keep it in a dry place.

Here are two modern version of potting meats for Beef and Ox Tongue:—

186. Potted Beef

2lb of lean beef, a pinch of allspice, mace and powdered cloves, salt and pepper, 1 teaspoon of anchovy essence, 2ozs clarified butter.

You will need for this a good stone jar or casserole that is deep and round. Trim and cut the meat into ½ inch pieces. Put them into a stone jar or casserole with 2 tablespoons of water, the mace, allspice, cloves, salt and pepper. Cover with greaseproof paper, then the lid and place this in a pan of boiling water. Cook gently for 3½ hours; replenishing the water as it reduces.

Then let it go warm, and pound the meat well, adding the juice from the meat and the anchovy essence little by little. Season to taste and rub through a sieve. Press it into clean pots and cover with the clarified butter.

187. Potted Ox Tongue Author's recipe

1 cooked ox tongue about 2lb in weight, 6ozs clarified butter, ¼ teaspoonful of mace, cloves, nutmeg, cayenne, black pepper and salt.

Chop the tongue very fine, then pound it well adding gradually 4ozs of the clarified butter, very slowly add the herbs and seasonings to taste. When the mixture is smooth, rub through a fine wire sieve, press into clean pots and cover with the 2ozs of clarified butter that is left.

188. Potting Salmon (1844)

Take *a large piece of fresh salmon,* scale it and wipe it clean. Then season it with *Jamaica pepper, black pepper, mace and cloves,* beat fine and mixed with *salt and a little sal-prunella:* then pour *clarified butter* over it and bake it well. When it is done take it out carefully and lay it on a cloth to drain. As soon as it is quite cold season it again, lay it close in your pot and cover it with clarified butter.

189. Potting Lobster (1868)

Boil a *live lobster in salt and water* and stick a skewer in the vent to prevent the water getting in. As soon as it is cold take out all the flesh, beat it fine in a mortar and season it with *beaten mace, grated nutmeg, pepper and salt.* Mix all together, melt *a piece of butter the size of a walnut* and mix it with the lobster as you beat it. When it is beaten to a paste put it into your pot and press it down as close and hard as you can. Then set some butter in a deep broad pan before the fire and when it is melted take off the scum at the top, if any, and pour the clear butter over the fish as thick as a crown piece. The whey and churn-milk will settle at the bottom of the pan; but take care that none of that goes in, and always let your butter be very good or you will spoil all. If you choose you may put the meat whole, with the body mixed among it, laying them as close together as you can and pouring the butter over them.

190. Potted Shrimps (1860)

This is a very popular dish so I thought I would add this to the recipes. It was very popular in the holiday resorts in the 1800's and Victoria herself was a great lover of the potted shrimp. This recipe is from Morecambe in the 1830's, but I have modernised it so that you can make it.

1lb of shrimps (shelled), salt and pepper, ground cloves and a ¼ teaspoon of cayenne, 6ozs of clarified butter.

Put the shrimps in a saucepan with the herbs and seasoning and 4ozs of clarified butter, and cook gently mixing well the herbs and butter for 3 minutes. Leave them to go just warm and then start potting them, the tighter the better, but be gentle enough not to cut them. Cover them with the rest of the clarified butter, let them set. Serve cold with lemon wedge and brown bread.

Chapter 45
A Happy Victorian Christmas

A Victorian Christmas was very much a family affair, where everyone exchanged presents, games and the odd joke. I will give you some of the recipes that were very popular then. We are used to turkey, chipolatas, brussels sprouts, carrots with roast and boiled potatoes. This seems to be the traditional British Christmas Dinner which even the poor families made sure was on the table over this festive season, also a bowl of grapes, dates, oranges and apples with an arrangement of flowers to decorate the table. Here is a typical Victorian Christmas menu.

191. Chestnut Soup
3 dozen chestnuts, 2ozs gammon diced, 1 large potato, 2 carrots, 1 bayleaf, 1½ stock, salt and pepper.
Shell the chestnuts and place them in salted water, bring to the boil. Peel them and put them into a saucepan with potato and carrots diced, add salt and pepper. Put enough stock on them and simmer until the chestnuts are quite tender. Then rub the carrots, potato and chestnuts through a sieve, put the puree into a saucepan and add the rest of the stock to thin the puree. Stir well, simmer for a few minutes and serve with croutons.

192. Salmon Cutlet with Hollandaise
2 inch slices of middle cut red salmon, seasoned well with salt and ground black pepper.
Butter a baking tray and place the salmon on the tray. Sprinkle with a little olive oil, and grill both sides until it comes away from the bone with ease. Serve with lemon and Hollandaise sauce.

Christmas Dinner *(Hannah Firmin)*.

193. Truffled Turkey

Today this would be very expensive with the price of fresh truffles, I suggest a stuffing of sausage meat and thyme as a poor substitute, unless you can afford the truffles.

1 turkey 7lbs (trussed), 1lb pork fat, 1lb truffles, 3 tablespoons of cherry brandy, 3 of Madeira, 3 tablespoons of olive oil, 1 teaspoon of thyme, 1 bayleaf crushed, a pinch of mixed spices, salt and pepper.

Wash the truffles thoroughly, and peel them very carefully. This applies to fresh truffles, and not the tinned or bottled which are ready for use. Keep 3 of the larger ones, which are cut into thin slices and slipped under the skin of the breast of the turkey. Cut the remaining truffles into quarters. Put them into a basin with the Madeira, brandy, oil, mixed spices and a little salt and let them stand in this mixture for an hour.

Cut the pork fat into small pieces, pound them or mince, warm slightly, then rub through a sieve with the peeling from the truffles. Now put it in a saucepan, on a low heat. When it is melted and barely warm add the truffles and their marinade. Mix well, then remove from the saucepan. When quite cold set, stuff the turkey with the mixture. Roast the turkey, basting with melted butter. Gas mark 3, 160C, 325F for 4 hours. Serve with bacon rolls and Cranberry Jelly.

194. Lamb in a Blanket (en Croûte)

4lb of leg of lamb (boned), 14ozs puff pastry, 1 egg beaten, rosemary, sage, salt and freshly ground black pepper.

Trim the lamb for excess fat, sprinkle with the rosemary, sage, salt and black pepper. Place the lamb in a roasting tin and cook in a preheated oven Gas 4, 350F for 1¾ hours, until almost cooked. Leave it to cool and increase the oven to Gas 7, 425F. Roll out the pastry to a rectangle 20×10 inches, 50×25cm. Brush the edges with beaten egg. Place the lamb in the centre of the pastry and fold it over to enclose the lamb completely. Trim and seal the edges well together. Decorate with diamond shapes from the trimmings and brush with beaten egg. Return to the oven and cook for 35 minutes until golden brown.

195. Christmas Plum Pudding

1½lb raisins, ½lb currants, ¾lb of fresh breadcrumbs, ½lb flour, ½lb beef suet, 9 eggs, 1 wineglass of good brandy, ½lb citron and orange peel, 3ozs sugar, ½ teaspoon of nutmeg, ½lb sultanas and a little ground ginger.

Mix the suet with the breadcrumbs and flour, add the sultanas, raisins, currants, citron and orange peel (wafer thin slices). Mix all well together with the grated nutmeg and ginger, then stir in the 9 eggs and brandy mixing well. Put the mixture into a buttered mould, tie it over with greaseproof paper and boil it for 6 hours. Serve with holly with brandy poured around in flames.

196. Spotted Dick

8ozs self-raising flour, 2 eggs, 6ozs currants, 4ozs butter, 2 tablespoons of castor sugar, a pinch of salt and a little milk.

Sift the flour with the salt into a basin, rubbing in the butter, and then add the currants and sugar blending in. Whisk the eggs and add to the mixture, stir until smooth adding a little milk. Place the mixture into a well greased basin, cover with greaseproof paper, tie securely and boil or steam for 2 hours.

The cost of making homemade mincepies for a family of six would not be cheap at today's prices. This recipe would have cost 6d in the 1850's.

197. Mincemeat (1850)

3 lemons, 3 apples, 1lb of raisins, ½lb currants, 1lb suet, 2lbs castor sugar, 1oz candied citron, 1oz candied orange peel, 1 wineglass of brandy and 2 tablespoons of orange marmalade.

Grate the rinds of the lemons, squeeze out the juice, strain it, and boil the remainder of the lemons until tender enough to chop very finely. Then add to this pulp the apples, which should be baked, and their skins and cores removed. Put in the remaining ingredients and mix very thoroughly together. Put the mincemeat into jars with tight lids and store for about two weeks before use.

Goose was also a very popular christmas dish with the Victorians, but because of the fat on a goose, truffle would be wasted if used in the same manner as turkey. Roast Ham, Ragout of Duck, Guinea Fowl and a Baron of Beef would also be found in the large households with trifles. Twelfth cake which we know as Christmas Cake was very rich and would have sovereigns in it if you were very wealthy.

198. Christmas Cake (1840) Twelfth Cake

2lbs of flour, 2lbs of best butter, 2lbs castor sugar, 20 eggs, 4lbs currants, 1lb sultanas, 1lb raisins, ½lb of sliced almonds, 1lb citron, ½lb orange candied peel, ½lb lemon candied peel, 1 tablespoon of ground nutmeg, ¼ of ginger, a little mixed spice, ½ teaspoon of ground cloves, ½ teaspoonful of cinnamon, ½lb glazed cherries, ½ glass of fine brandy, ¼ glass of best port, and a ¼ glass of the best British sherry, rind and juice of 2 lemons.

Work the butter to a smooth cream. Sift all the dry ingredients — flour, spices and almonds — together into a large bowl. Mix in all the chopped fruits and blend thoroughly. Mix together to a smooth paste the butter, sugar and lemon rind, beat in the eggs one at a time. Stir this into the flour and fruit mixture, add lemon juice and pour the brandy, port and sherry in very slowly. Let this mixture stand for 4 hours. Butter two 12 inch round cake tins thoroughly; line them with a double layer of greaseproof paper brushed with melted butter. Tie a layer of paper around the outside of the tins, allowing it to protrude well above the rim — this prevents the cake from burning during baking.

Spoon the mixture into the prepared tin, level the top and bake the cakes on the shelf below the centre of the oven, at mark 2, 300F for 2 hours. Reduce the heat to 250F (gas ½) and bake for a further 4 hours. When cool and stood for at least 3 hours wrap the cakes in tin foil and store one until Christmas, keeping the other to one side for a wedding or birthday cake.

This recipe is a modern version of the 1840's twelfth cake. If you are placing coins in cakes always be sure to boil them in salt water first, then foil them. Always let your guests know that you have inserted coins in the cake for safety of children.

Top the cake with your favourite glaze, (peach or apricot), roll out 3lb almond paste and cover the cake completely. Then make up 3 lb of Royal Icing and decorate to your own theme.

Christmas Sauces

With sauces being my favourite subject and Christmas being party time, I love to experiment. So I thought I would give you two of my favourite recipes as well as the famous Brandy Sauce and Bread Sauce for the turkey.

199. Bread Sauce 1868

1 large onion, 6 cloves, 1 pint of milk, 1oz butter, 6ozs fresh breadcrumbs, salt and black pepper to taste, a teaspoon of fresh chives.

Stud the onion with the cloves and put into a pan with the milk, add the salt and pepper, and just bring to the boiling point. Remove the pan from the heat and leave the onion to infuse for 40 minutes. Add the breadcrumbs and butter, mix well and cook gently for 20 minutes stirring occasionally. Remove the onion, take out the cloves, chop very fine and add to the sauce with the fresh chives.

200. Yuletide Sauce for Game (Author's recipe)

½ pint of Madeira, 1½ tablespoons clarified butter, 1½ tablespoons flour, ½ pint of good brown stock or consomme, a teaspoon of crushed fennel seed, 2 tablespoons of tarragon vinegar, salt and freshly ground black pepper.

If you enjoy sauces then you will find a peppermill a must for the art of good sauces.

Melt the butter and stir in the flour, then cook over a low heat until the mixture is pale brown. Slowly add the Madeira and stock, bring to the boil. Add the herbs, seasoning and tarragon vinegar, simmer for 40 minutes, stirring occasionally. Skim and strain the sauce. This sauce is excellent with Venison ribs or Wild Duck.

201. Brandy Sauce 1875

1 teaspoon of arrowroot, ¼ pint of milk, 3 tablespoons of fine brandy, 1 teaspoon of soft brown sugar, 1 teaspoon of castor sugar and 1 egg yolk.

Mix the arrowroot with a little cold milk. Put a ¼ pint of milk in a medium saucepan and when boiling stir in the arrowroot, bring the milk back to boiling point, mixing in the egg yolk, sugar and brandy when the milk has cooled a little. Not until then cook, without boiling, until the yolk thickens and it is a golden colour in respect of it being milky.

202. We Three Kings Sauce (Author's recipe)

½ pint of strawberry yoghurt, 2 tablespoons of clear honey, 1 teaspoon of lemon juice, ¼ pint of water, ½oz cornflour blended with 1 tablespoon of your favourite liqueur.

Put the yoghurt into a saucepan bring to the boil and add the lemon juice, honey and water, let it simmer for 5 minutes then add the cornflour with your favourite liqueur. I made this after making a chocolate rum souffle from the *Robert Carrier Cookbook* in 1975. I thought they went together beautifully.

Chapter 44
A special Four Course Meal

To close the book, I have compiled a four course meal combining the talents of, perhaps, the most famous people in the catering trade in the 19th century. All the dishes have been modernised, so you too can impress your family and friends with the dishes that pleased thousands in those bygone days when food was glorious.

203. Lentil Soup (Mrs Beeton 1861)
1 lb of lentils, 2ozs butter, 1½ pints of good pork or veal stock, 2 cloves of garlic, 1 large sliced onion, salt and freshly ground white pepper to taste.
Boil the lentils in a large saucepan for 20 minutes, then pour off the water, add a small quantity of fresh with the butter and seasoning and simmer until quite soft. Stir in the stock and add the garlic and (fried off) onion. Simmer for 2 hours.

204. Soles au Gratin (Alexis Soyer 1836)
1 large sole, 1 tablespoon of brown breadcrumbs, juice of ½ lemon, 2 teaspoons of chopped onions, half glass of white wine, 1 glass of fish stock, 1 teaspoon of chopped mushroom, 1 teaspoon of chopped parsley, 1 essence of anchovy, 1 teaspoon of sugar and 1 teaspoon of cayenne, ¼ pint of demi-glace (brown sauce), butter.
Trim and skin the sole, make an incision in the back, then add a knob of butter in a saute-pan with 2 teaspoonfuls of chopped onions and ½ glass of white wine. Lay the sole in the pan and cover it with demi-glace, breadcrumbs and a few more knobs of butter.

Place in a moderate oven for 25 minutes. Take it out of the saute-pan, and place it on a dish. Then put the glass of stock in the saute-pan with a little demi-glace, and boil it for 7 minutes stirring all the time. When it has reduced by ⅓, add the juice of half a lemon, parsley, mushroom, essence of anchovy, cayenne and sugar. Pour the sauce round the fish, place it again in the oven for 15 minutes, then under the grill for 2 minutes. Serve with lemon and chopped parsley.

205. Breast of Chicken with Foie Gras & Madeira
(Auguste Escoffier)

4 chicken breasts, 2ozs butter, croutons, 4 small slices foie gras sauteed in butter, white stock, 3 tablespoons Madeira, 4 tablespoons of meat jelly, truffle.

Cook the 4 chicken fillets dipped in flour in butter until golden brown on both sides, arrange on croutons and put a slice of foie gras on each fillet. Add a little stock to the butter left in the pan in which the fillets were cooked, and mix well. Add the Madeira and meat jelly, and bring to the boil slowly for a few minutes. Add some thin slices of truffle, allowing 4 slices for each fillet. Boil for a further 3 minutes, then add 1 oz butter and pour over the chicken.

206. Stewed Cucumbers (William Kitchener, 1817)

2 large cucumbers peeled, sliced, 4 tablespoons of flour, 1oz butter, 2 tablespoons of oil, ½ pint of chicken stock and 2 tablespoons of parsley, 10 small onions.

Place the cucumber slices lightly in the flour. Brown them with the onions in the butter and oil mixed. Season with salt and ground black pepper. Add the stock, cover and simmer for 10 minutes. Sprinkle with the chopped parsley.

207. Tomatoes Stuffed with Mushrooms (Eliza Acton 1845)

¼lb button mushrooms, 1oz butter, 1oz fine breadcrumbs, a little cayenne pepper, a little stock, and 8 ripe tomatoes (firm), salt and pepper to taste.

Slice the tops off the tomatoes and scoop out the insides. Sieve the pulp and mix with the breadcrumbs, butter cut into small pieces, cayenne, salt and pepper. Add the mushrooms. Fill the tomatoes with the mixture and bake in the oven for 15 minutes in a moderate oven Gas 4 350°.

208. Rosa's Potatoes Author (for Rosa Lewis)

6 cold boiled potatoes (in skins), 2ozs butter, 1 teaspoon of flour, ¼ pint of double cream, 2 tablespoons of toasted sesame seeds, 2 tablespoons of chives, salt and pepper, 3 tablespoons of brown breadcrumbs.

Peel and dice the potatoes, saute in the butter till brown. Add the chives, salt, pepper and flour, slowly add the cream, let it cook for 3 minutes. Sprinkle with the breadcrumbs and sesame seed and grill for 1 minute.

209. Apple Charlotte (Marie Antoine Careme 1828)

*2lb cooking apples, 3 tablespoons of castor sugar, juice of 1
lemon, 2ozs butter, 3 tablespoons of water, 4 tablespoons of
apricot puree (or jam), bread.*

Butter a charlotte mould. Cut out some star shaped croutons of
bread, about ½ inch thick. Dip them into melted butter and
arrange them in the bottom of the mould, overlapping each other.
Cut some oblong pieces of bread of the same thickness and height
as the mould, dip them into melted butter and line the sides of the
mould overlapping again.

Put the apples peeled and sliced into a saucepan with ½oz butter,
lemon juice, sugar and water. Cook until it has reduced to a thick
pulp and stir in the apricot puree or jam. Fill the mould with the
mixture, making sure the mould is full. Cover with more slices of
bread dipped in melted butter. Bake in a moderate oven 35 mins.

210. Apricot Sauce (Anthelme Brillat-Savarin 1820)

Put *10 ripe apricots* through a sieve and puree, put the pulp into a
copper pan and dilute with ½ *pint of light syrup,* bring to the boil
adding a tot of *kirsch, and cherry brandy liqueur.* Remove from the
heat when the sauce coats the spoon.

Note 1
Weights and Measures

The weights and measures contained in the recipes are English.

Measures of Weight
20 grains = 1 scruple = 20grs
3 scruples = 1 drachm = 60grs.
8 drachms = 1 ounce = 480 grs.
16 ounces = 1 pound = 7,680 grs.

Metric Equivalents
1oz = 30 grammes
½lb (8ozs) = 225 grammes
1lb (16ozs) = 453.5 grammes
2.205lb = 1 kilogramme
Fluid
½ Imperial pint = 2518 decilitres
1¾ Imperial pints = 1 litre

Measures of Capacity
60 minims = 1 fluid drachm
8 fluid drachms = 1 fluid ounce
20 fluid ounces = 1 pint
8 pints = 1 gallon

Liquid Measures
2 tablespoons = ¼ gill
4 tablespoons = ½ gill
6 tablespoons = ¾ gill
8 tablespoons = 1 gill =
  5 fluid ounces = ¼ pint
4 gills = 20 fluid ounces = 1 pint
2 pints = 1 quart
4 quarts = 1 gallon

Abbreviations
The following abbreviations are used throughout the book.
sp.   spoonful
teasp. teaspoonful
oz.   ounce
lb.   pound
min.   minute
in.   inch
hr.   hour
pt.   pint
qt.   quart

Note 2
Cook's Oven Guide

Few ovens are accurately adjusted. If you are not satisfied with the results given by your oven, test the temperature range with an oven thermometer and set your dial accordingly.

Oven Temperature Chart

	Fahr	Cent	Gas Mark
Very Cool	225	110	¼
	250	130	½
Cool	275	140	1
	300	150	2
Moderate	325	170	3
	350	180	
Moderately hot	375	190	5
	400	200	6
Hot	425	220	7
	450	230	8
Very Hot	475	240	9

Note 3
Cooking Methods and Terms

Allemande: reduced white veloute sauce thickened with cream and yolks of eggs, seasoned with nutmeg and lemon juice.

Angelica: a plant preserved in syrup, and used for decorating pastry etc.

Aspic Jelly: a transparent jelly made from meat and used for garnishing etc.

Au bleu: fish dressed so as to present a bluish appearance.

Au gratin: a dish which is coated with sauce, sprinkled with cheese or breadcrumbs and browned in the oven or under the grill.

Baba: a very light plum cake.

Bain Marie: a square tin cooking utensil, with a loose bottom. A kind of very shallow cistern, to be placed on a hot hearth. It contains hot water in which vessels containing soup etc., are placed, that they may be kept warm without being longer subject to the action of the fire, which would reduce or thicken them.

Baking: cooking by dry heat in the oven.

Bard: a substitute for larding, when the assistance of fat is needed in dressing any substance i.e. bard is a thin slice of bacon fat which is put over the breasts of birds, back of hare, etc.

Basting: moisten food with fat or other liquids while cooking.

Beating: Whipping motion, using a fork, whisk or beater in order to introduce air into the mixture to make it smooth and light.

Bechamel: French white sauce.

Beignet: a fritter.

Bisque: a shell fish soup.

Blanc: a white broth used instead of water for boiling chickens, etc., to make them white in appearance.

Blanch: to put the substance to be done in cold water, boil it, strain it and plunge it into cold water. Also to remove the outside skin of almonds.

Blanquettes: thin slices of white meat warmed in white sauce, thickened with the yolk of eggs.

Blending: mixing 2 or more ingredients that each loses its identity.

Boudin: an entrée prepared with quenelle forcemeat.

Bouilli: a stew of beef, served with sauce.

Bouillon: broth

Bouquet of Herbs: parsley, thyme and green onions tied together.

Bouquet garni: mixture of herbs tied in a muslin and used to flavour soups, stews and sauces.

Braise: a kind of compound used for giving flavour to braised meats, and for keeping poultry etc., white while braising.

Braising: a mode of stewing with bacon.

Brioche: a spongy cake resembling Bath buns.

Callispash: the glutinous meat of the upper shell of the turtle.

Calipee: The glutinous meat of the under shell of the same creature.

Caramel: sugar boiled till the water is all evaporated, and used for ornamentation.

Casserole: a stew pan.

Casserole: a rice crust made in the shape of a pie.

Chartreuse of Vegetables: a preparation of vegetables arranged in a plain mould, the interior garnished with game, fillets, tendons, etc.

Clarifying: butter, skimmed and strained, to be used in sauces etc.

Compote: stewed fruit and syrup; or stewed pigeons, etc.

Consommé: a strong gravy left from stewing meat.

Coulis: a rich brown gravy.

Croquantes: bright mixtures of fruit and boiled sugar.

Croquettes: A savoury mince of fish, meat, etc., formed into shapes and fried.

Croustade: a kind of patty.

Croûtons: various shapes of fried or toasted bread.

Daube: meat or fowl stewed in sauce.

Desosser: to bone.

En papilotte (in paper): putting a cutlet into an oiled or buttered paper.

Entrée: a side dish for the first course.

Entremet: a corner dish for second course.

Escalopes: collops.

Espagnole: a brown sauce, the foundation of most other sauces.

Faggot: a tiny bunch of parsley, thyme and a bayleaf tied together.

Farce: forcemeat or stuffing.

Folding: method of combining beaten egg whites or whipped cream with another mixture so that the air cells are not broken down.

Foncer: to lay ham, veal or bacon at the bottom of a saucepan under meat.

Fricandeau: a made dish of boned and larded veal.

Galette: a peculiar French Cake.

Gâteau: a cake.

Glacé: coated with a thin syrup or butter glaze.

Glaze: stock boiled down to a thin paste.

Godiveaux: different kinds of forcemeat.

Grilling: to cook food under a flame rather than over a flame.

Jardinière: a preparation of vegetables stewed down in their own sauce.

Kneading: a method of pressing, folding and stretching dough with the hands.

Lardoon: the piece of bacon used in larding.

Leason: a mixture of egg and cream.

Lit: a layer.

Luting: a paste to fasten the lids on pie pans for preserving game.

Maigre: dishes for fast days made without flesh.

Marinade: a liquor for boiling or stewing meat or fish in.

Matelote: a rich stew made of fish and wine.

Mayonnaise: cold salad dressing.

Mignonnette Pepper: pepper corns ground coarsely.

Miroton: pieces of meat not larger than a crown piece made into a ragout.

Nougat: a mixture of almonds and sugar.

Nouilles: a kind of vermicelli.

Paner: to put breadcrumbs.

Poële: a kind of broth made of veal, bacon, etc, used to boil fowls in.

Pot au feu: the stock pot.

Profiteroles: a light kind of pastry creamed inside.

Purée: a thick soup.

To Purée: reducing one or a combination of cooked foods to a smooth pulp by putting them through a muslin or sieve.

Roux: melted butter or fat combined with an equal amount of flour and used as a basis for the thickening of soups, gravies and sauces.

Quenelles: forcemeat of meat, fish, etc., formed into balls and fried.

Ragout: a very rich sauce or made dish.

Rissoles: balls of minced meat covered with egg and breadcrumbs then fried.

Salmis: a hash of half-roasted game.

Sauce Piquante: an acid sauce.

To Sauté: cooking small pieces of vegetable or meat very gently in a little fat or butter until they are tender, but not browned.

Seasoning: three bay leaves, six cloves, a blade or two of mace, pepper and salt.

Simmering: a word used quite a lot in this book. To cook a food or liquid, which is kept just below boiling point for a period of time.

Soufflé: the very lightest of puddings; a puffed up pudding.

Stewing: the process of cooking food slowly in enough liquid to cover the food, in a closed pot until tender.

Steeping: process of soaking various foods in a liquid preparation.

Stock: fat or lean stock, vegetable or meat juices used for sauces, stews or braising.

Strainer: kitchen utensil used for straining sauces.

Terrine: earthenware dish in which game, fish or meat are cooked. The word terrine is also used to designate the food itself; for example terrine of chicken.

Turbans and Mazarines: ornamental entrées of forced meat, fillets of poultry or fish.

Tureen: broad, deep dish in which soup is served, not to be confused with the above.

Velouté: name given to a white sauce made with veal or chicken stock, also used to describe certain thickened soups.

Vinaigrette: mixture of vinegar and oil seasoned with salt and pepper, with chopped herbs.

Vol au Vent: very light puff pastry formed into cups and filled with ragoût or mince.

Zeste: French word for peel, the exterior, coloured part of the skin of lemon, orange and tangerine for flavour.

Note 4
Seasons of Food

Butchers Meat
Beef: all year round
Lamb: spring and summer
Mutton: all year
Veal: all year
Pork: September to 1st May

Poultry
Chicken: all year round
Turkey: all year round
Spring chicken: spring
Goose: autumn — winter
Gosling: September
Guinea-fowl: all year round
Duck: all year round
Duckling: April — June

Game
Grouse: 12th August
— 9th December
Partridge: September — 1st
February
Pheasant: October — 1st February
Ptarmigan: August — December
Quail: all year round
Wild Duck: September — March
Woodcock: September — March
Wood-pigeon: August — March
Venison: (male) May — September
(female) September — January
Rabbit: autumn to spring
Hare: August to 1st March

Fish
Barbel: June — March
Cod: best May to February
Eel: all year round
Haddock: all year round
Halibut: all year round
Hake: September to February
Herring: better September to April
John Dory: January to July
Lemon Sole: October to March
Mackerel: March to August
Plaice: better May to January
Salmon: February to September
Sole: all year round
Trout: March to October (river)
Turbot: all year round
Whiting: August to February is best

Shellfish
Crab: summer
Crayfish: October to March
Lobster: summer
Mussel: September to May
Oysters: 1st September to 1st May
Prawn: September to May
Scallop: September to April
Shrimp: all year round
Snail: September to April

Vegetables
Artichoke: (Jerusalem) October to
March
Artichoke: (globe) better summer
to autumn
Asparagus: May to July
Broad Beans: July to August
Broccoli: October to April
Cabbage: all year round
Carrots: all year round
Cauliflower: all year round
Celery: August to March
Chicory: better in winter
Cucumber: all year round (better
in summer)
Egg-plant: (aubergine) summer
French beans: May to September
Leek: October to March
Lettuce: all year round (better
in summer)
Mushroom: all year round
Onion: all year round
Parsnip: October to March
Pea: June to September
Radish: better in the summer
Runner bean: July to September
Shallot: September to February
Spinach: all year round
Swede: December to March
Sweetcorn: summer to autumn
Tomato: all year round (better in
summer)
Turnip: October to March
Vegetable marrow: July to
October

201

Index of recipes

See also recipe no 184

169. Summer salad
170. Salad de légumes

Jams, Chutneys, Jellies and
Pickles
171. Blackberry and apple jam
172. Cherry jam
173. Rhubarb jam
174. Lemon curd
175. Tangerine marmalade
176. Apple chutney
177. Piccalilli
178. Tomato chutney
179. Apple jelly
180. Damson jam
181. Medlar jelly
182. Mint jelly
183. Lemon pickle

Pot dishes
184. Potting venison
185. Potting beef
186. Potted beef
187. Potted ox tongue
188. Potting salmon
189. Potting lobster
190. Potted shrimps

Christmas Recipes
191. Chestnut soup
192. Salmon cutlet with hollandaise
193. Truffled turkey
194. Lamb in a blanket
195. Christmas plum pudding
196. Spotted dick
197. Mincemeat
198. Christmas cake
199. Bread sauce
200. Yuletide sauce for game
201. Brandy sauce
202. We Three Kings sauce

Special Four Course Meal
203. Lentil soup
204. Soles au Gratin
205. Breast of chicken with foie gras
        and madeira
206. Stewed cucumbers
207. Tomatoes stuffed with mushrooms
208. Rosa's potatoes
209. Apple Charlotte
210. Apricot Sauce

Bibliography

Warnes Model Cookery & Housekeeping Book, Mary Jewry (1868)

The Caterer & Refreshment Contractors Gazette (1878)

The Frugal Housewife & Young Woman's Companion, William Street, (1811)

The Forme of Cury (1385)

The Book of Household Management & Everyday Cookery, Isabella Beeton 1861 & 1876

The Cooks Oracle, Dr William Kitchener (1817)

The English Bread Book & Modern Cookery in all branches, Eliza Acton 1845

Dinners and Dinner Parties, G.V. (1862)

The Physiology of Taste, Brillat Savarin

The Domestic Cookery 1806, 1843 and 1878

Enquire Within 1891

The History of England (1883)

Chronological History of Bolton, James Clegg (1800)

The Woman's Companion (1806)

Common Sense Management of the Stomach, George Drewry M.D. (1875)

Le Guide Culinaire, Auguste Escoffier

L'Art de la Cuisine Francais, Anton Careme

The Modern Housewife & Shilling Cookery, Alexis Soyer

The Complete Herbalist, Prof. O. Phelps Brown (1897)

The People of Bolton on Cookery, Tom Bridge 1982

General Index